Praise for *The Christmas Devotional*

"What a fabulous book to snuggle up with during the busyness of the holiday season! When minds are filled with gift-buying, decorating, and seasonal baking, wrap your heart around *The Christmas Devotional: Hope & Humor for the Holidays.* Michelle Medlock Adams and Andy Clapp remind you of the true meaning of Christmas with poignant messages, laughter, and maybe even a few nostalgic and redemptive tears. A must-read for Christmastime. Grab a blanket and some cocoa and cuddle up with this devo every morning or evening and you'll be rejuvenated and ready to face the holiday to-do list each day!"

—JULIE LAVENDER, award-winning author of *Children's Bible Stories for Bedtime* (Zeitgeist/Penguin Random House) and *365 Ways to Love Your Child: Turning Little Moments into Lasting Memories* (Revell).

"If you're looking for a folksy downhome read this Christmas, Michelle and Andy have just what you're looking for. This devotional is sure to put some tingle in your jingle! I know you'll love the stories of family, faith, and friendship as much as I did."

—LARRY DUGGER, Bestselling author, pastor, and life coach

"*The Christmas Devotional: Hope & Humor for the Holidays* by Michelle Medlock Adams and Andy Clapp will sit on my decorated table next to the singing Snowman playing the piano. This adorable and well-crafted devotional ranks up there with the 12 Days of Christmas and needs to be a part of the holiday season. It's filled with wonderful chapters that combine inspiration and a solid Christian message with festive fun facts about Christmas. Day 4 deals with the colors of Christmas and delivers a powerful message about God's love for you and me. And then Michelle tosses in a tidbit about the history of the inventor of the electric Christmas lights. Brilliant! These little facts, like the one when Andy writes about how many pounds of wax are used to produce candles each year in the United States, are peppered throughout this 40-day Christmas journey. He wrapped up Day 9 where he wrote about how God is the light in the darkness. This book has it all and will put you in the Christmas mood weeks before the Big Day! Bravo Michelle and Andy."

—DEL DUDUIT, Award-winning author of more than a dozen inspirational books

End Game Press books may be purchased in bulk at special discounts for sales promotion, corporate gifts, ministry, fund-raising, or educational purposes. Special editions can also be created to specifications. For details, contact Special Sales Dept., End Game Press, P.O. Box 206, Nesbit, MS 38651 or info@endgamepress.com.

Visit our website at www.endgamepress.com.

Library of Congress Control Number: 2023930689
Hardback ISBN: 978-1-63797-094-2
eBook ISBN: 978-1-63797-095-9

Cover design by Bruce Gore, Gore Studio Inc. Interior design by Monica Thomas for TLC Book Design, TLCBookDesign.com. Cover images by iStock Images, istockphoto.com and Shutterstock, shutterstock.com. Interior images from various contributors, including Adobe Stock, stock.adobe.com and Deposit Photos, depositphotos.com; photos on pages 11, 113 courtesy of Michelle Medlock Adams; image of St. Nicholas "Lipensky" on page 122, by Aleksa Petrov, Public Domain, CC0.

Published in association with Cyle Young of the Cyle Young Literary Elite, LLC.

Printed in the USA
10 9 8 7 6 5 4 3 2

The
Christmas
Devotional

Hope & Humor for the Holidays

MICHELLE MEDLOCK ADAMS
and ANDY CLAPP

Table of Contents

Celebrating Christmas in the Summer

By Andy Clapp

The majesty of the holiday season needs more than a month of celebration.

As the temperature creeps upwards on the thermometer, a heart that beats for the Christmas chill longs for a reprieve. Thankfully, Christmas in July celebrations interrupt the almost eternal pause between last Christmas and a Christmas yet to come.

I adore Christmas. Christmas has always warmed my heart. Of all the celebrations of the year, it stands as my favorite. I could live in a Christmas store and never tire of the lights, smells, and overall festiveness. As summer classes carried on, my heart ached for something Christmas.

In the summer of 1999, my heart found inspiration. ABC Family introduced me to the phenomenon known as "Christmas in July." Flipping through the channels one humid North Carolina day in July, my eyes fell on a Christmas movie. Joy rose up from the depth of my soul. Hope overcame the humidity! When the first movie ended, another began.

It was as if the skies parted and a hallelujah chorus began. A week's worth of programming promised an interruption to the summer, a respite from the mundane.

I tore out of the rental house.

"Dude, where are you going?" Rob, my roommate, asked as we passed each other in the driveway.

"I gotta get some blank VCR tapes."

He looked befuddled.

"I just found Christmas movies on TV. I'm going to tape them all!"

He grinned. He understood the depth of my passion for all things Christmas.

I bought twelve tapes and filled nearly every one.

As the years progressed, more Christmas in July events became mid-year pick-me-ups for my soul as it suffered through Christmas withdrawals. Minor league baseball teams held Christmas in July nights, so I took the family to the ballpark to see the Christmas trees and greet Santa. Each year the small town of West Jefferson, North Carolina held a Christmas in July festival. Each year, we ran to the hills to enjoy the streets lined with vendors and the music filling the air. The feeling of Christmas washed over my soul.

Deep inside us, there is a longing to feel the warmth of Christmas throughout the year. As we live in a cold and calloused world, the Spirit of Christmas brings us relief. The heart of Christmas reminds us of a hope that exists in every season. Sometimes, we just need a diversion from the norm when Christmas feels so far away.

What began as a normal night in a field two thousand years ago transitioned in an instant into something more. Shepherds watched the flocks until their focus shifted. A light pierced the darkness as an angel brought news of the birth of the Savior. Suddenly, one angel became a multitude. Glory filled the air and the praise of God rained down from the heavens. A holy interruption from above set the hearts of the shepherds ablaze. Everything changed.

They set out to find the One they'd heard had come. In Bethlehem, in a stable of all places, there He lay. The interruption of the night led to a transformation of their entire lives and their situation. Their plans gave way to God's miracle. Their schedule cast aside as they made an unplanned journey.

The rigors of life in general lock us into routines. Mired in the routines, we miss what a glorious life we live in Jesus. Our hearts grow heavy. Our minds become engulfed in the fog of the world. As the year wears on, we miss the beauty of Christmas until a God-sized interruption reminds us of what He did in Bethlehem and what it means for our lives.

When life gets thrown off-balance, bemoaning the unscheduled event can be an option. Or, we can look to see why God allowed the unexpected to take place.

To rescue us from the mundane, dog days of life, He sometimes breaks in to refresh our hearts and minds.

> **FESTIVE FUN FACTS**
>
> Ashe County, the location of West Jefferson's Christmas in July festival, is also the largest producer of Christmas trees in the nation. Ashe County produces nearly two million trees each year, according to the Washington Post.[1]

Hearth to Heaven

"Heavenly Father, help us to carry the Spirit with us throughout the year. When we get too far removed, we ask You to break in and bring us back to the wonder and majesty of Jesus's coming. In Jesus' name we pray, Amen."

A GIFT FROM GOD

"Praise the God and Father of our Lord Jesus Christ. According to His great mercy, He has given us a new birth into a living hope through the resurrection of Jesus Christ from the dead and into an inheritance that is imperishable, uncorrupted, and unfading, kept in heaven for you."

1 PETER 1:3-4, HCSB

Holiday Hallmark Movies and Happy Endings

By Michelle Medlock Adams

I love this time of year for many reasons—celebrating the birth of Jesus, gathering with friends and family, baking, and eating Christmas cookies, giving, and receiving presents, decorating our home with lights and greenery, singing Christmas carols, and...watching all of the Hallmark Christmas movies.

Yes, I admit it—I'm obsessed with Hallmark holiday movies. And I have the "This is my Hallmark Christmas Movies Watching Shirt" to prove it, which I wear proudly with my light-up Christmas ornament earrings.

I even downloaded the Hallmark Christmas Movie app on my phone last year so that I wouldn't miss a single mistletoe-laden movie. I DVR my favorites, and then I watch those sappy Christmas movies all year long. (Currently, my favorite is *A Crown for Christmas* starring Danica McKellar. It came out in 2015, but it is still my go-to Hallmark Christmas flick.)

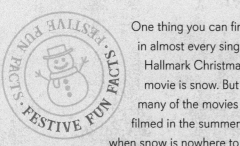

One thing you can find in almost every single Hallmark Christmas movie is snow. But many of the movies are filmed in the summer when snow is nowhere to be found. So how do they do it? How do they achieve a wintry wonderland?

According to a *Mental Floss* article by Jake Rossen, producers use several tricks to simulate snowfall such as: snow blankets that look quite real; foam; crushed limestone; commercial replica snow; and ice shavings. And sometimes for the closeups of the actors, producers might opt for soapy bubbles to mimic snow. Achieving authentic-looking snow isn't an inexpensive feat, which is why about $50,000 is budgeted for snow in each Christmas movie.[2]

True, the Hallmark Christmas movies are sometimes silly and almost always corny, but there's something else they all have in common that keeps me coming back for more—happy endings. (In Hallmark movies, there are none of those surprise sad "Nicholas Sparks" type endings.) By the end of a Hallmark flick, two high school sweethearts are reunited; or a little boy who once was hopeless discovers the true meaning of Christmas; or an estranged mother and daughter find their way back to each other just in time for Christmas morning. Sure, every single story features some sort of conflict, but each conflict is resolved in the most miraculous way within the next ninety minutes, leaving me with a smile on my face and a warm feeling in my heart.

I realize most Hallmark movies are not very believable and that's one of the reasons I like them so much. I know that in real life, high school sweethearts don't always reunite; and children don't always learn about the true meaning of Christmas; and families don't always make up and spend Christmas morning together. But I also know that even though life on this earth can be difficult and messy and painful at times, as Christians we are promised the Happy Ending of all happy endings. The Ultimate Happy Ending!

Because Jesus came to earth as a baby, lived a flawless life, died on a cross for our sins, and rose again, we get to spend eternity in heaven with Him where we'll experience happiness like we've never known before.

Even Hallmark can't top that happy ending!

Hearth to Heaven

"Lord, I acknowledge that I have sinned, and I come to You right now confessing that sin and asking for Your forgiveness. Thank You, Jesus, for dying on the cross for my sins. I believe You are the Son of God, and I believe that You rose from the dead and are alive today. I receive You right now as my Lord and Savior. Thank You for this new beginning and thank You that I am now guaranteed a happy ending in heaven with You. I love You, Lord. In the Mighty Name of Jesus, Amen."

A GIFT FROM GOD

"For this is how God loved the world: He gave his one and only Son, so that everyone who believes in him will not perish but have eternal life."

JOHN 3:16, NLT

Finding Meaning in the Majesty of the Season

By Andy Clapp

Do we know what it means?

Each year, we spend money, time, and energy transforming the ordinary into the extraordinary. Decorations add life and light to the interior and exterior of our old country church. Understanding these symbols adds life and light into the lives of those inside our spiritual community.

A sense of reverence rises in the service. The house of worship takes on an added layer of beauty. For our church, whose history extends back two hundred years, the décor at Christmas amazes all who enter.

Each stained-glass window features greenery and candles in the windowsill.

Garland hangs above the choir loft, as does a lighted star.

Dozens of vibrant poinsettias, wrapped in shiny green foil, cover the altar and the railings that encase the pulpit.

The green Christmas wreaths, wrapped in red ribbon, stand out as they adorn the old, white wooden doors welcoming you into the building

All these seasonal additions speak of a God who kept—and continues to keep—His promise. Humanity needed a Savior. God sent one to a stable of all places.

The Hanging of the Green service draws a crowd to sing the songs of the season while we decorate the church. Each person enjoys a role.

Our musicians offer special music while selected members read passages that help tell the story of the decorations and their attachment to Christmas.

Some hang wreaths.

Others place the candles in the windows.

Each family comes forward as a family unit to hang ornaments on the tree.

Isaiah and Micah's prophecies lead us into worship. God spoke through the prophets to give hope to His people. As the service continues, we reflect on the promise kept and the love shown then and now.

Understanding leads to a greater appreciation of each element. The tree holds meaning. The lights signify Jesus as the light of the world. As worshippers enter during this season, they are immersed in the wonder of Christmas. Their eyes absorb the symbols while the decorations blanket their souls with joy. Christmas—a celebration of Christ's arrival, a reflection on God's enduring love.

The Hanging of the Green service's history is somewhat unknown. Though difficult to trace its beginnings, many of the teachings within can be sourced. Martin Luther's thoughts on the Christmas tree date back to the sixteenth century, when he placed candles on his own tree. The pastor tells the stories of the hymns sung, teaching the congregants about each one's origin. Over time, all the elements weave together to teach more about the everlasting reason we have to celebrate Christmas.

The service centers the focus on Christ. Before the hustle and bustle of the world overwhelms even the most dedicated Christian, the Hanging of the Green sets a peaceful tone for the soul.

Thankfully, the service includes all ages. Families sit together. They decorate together. They grow together.

Scripture tells us that Mary held tight to the moments and the meaning.

She knew every aspect of her Son's birth held significance.

As the shepherds shared what happened, Luke pointed out Mary's reaction: *"But Mary was treasuring up all these things in her heart and meditating on them"* (Luke 2:19, HCSB). What happened captivated her heart like nothing before.

Every word spoken accentuated the majesty.

Her Son, the Son of God, came to the earth.

Angels delivered messages. Shepherds journeyed to see the Child. A mother held tight to every word, not just for a season, but for the rest of her life.

Later, Magi arrived bearing specific gifts. Gold, frankincense, and myrrh pointed to their understanding of the Child they bowed before.

To all, it was more than just another season. The birth of Christ stands as more than just a birth.

What does it mean to us? Is Christmas just a celebration, or do we carry the deeper meaning throughout life? When we understand the symbols, the beauty of Christmas becomes breathtaking.

Find a Hanging of the Green service in your area. Start such a service at your church. You will find even more joy during this time when you reflect on what it means before the season hits its pinnacle.

Christmas speaks of the nature of God. Hearing the message emphasizes the miracle of Bethlehem. Every symbol of Christmas calls out to your soul to know a love that extends beyond the season.

Each church exists to lead others to a deeper understanding of God. As Christmas draws more in attendance than any other time of the year, the Hanging of the Green opens the door for the church to fulfill that calling.

Sample Hanging of the Green Service

A Hope for Humanity
Reading of Isaiah 7, Isaiah 9, and Micah 5

Song
O Come, O Come Emmanuel

The Purpose of the Service
Wreaths: Reading on the meaning of the shape and use of evergreens for the wreaths. As the reading is conducted, selected worshippers hang wreaths on the doors of the church.

Song
O Come All Ye Faithful

Candles

Reading of John 1. As the reading is conducted, greenery and candles are placed in each windowsill.

Christmas Tree

Explanation of the importance of the tree
As an instrumental O Holy Night is played following the reading, families approach as family units to place their ornaments on the tree

Nativity Set

As the Nativity set is placed on the front table, each piece is explained.

Song

Joy to the World

The Christmas Story

Children come to the front. The Christmas Story is read from Luke 2.

The Legend of the Candy Cane

The Legend is read to the children, then each child receives a candy cane.

Message

Lighting of the Candles and Lighting of the Tree

Song

Silent Night

Benediction

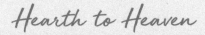

Hearth to Heaven

"Dear Heavenly Father, keep our eyes and our minds focused on You this Christmas season and beyond. May we be overwhelmed by the gift You gave to us as You sent Your Son to this world to die for our sins. Take us to Bethlehem this Christmas and help us to keep Christ at the heart of our celebration this season."

A GIFT FROM GOD

"Bethlehem Ephrathah, you are small among the clans of Judah;
One will come from you to be ruler over Israel for Me.
His origin is from antiquity, from eternity."

MICAH 5:2, HCSB

The Colors of Christmas

By Michelle Medlock Adams

Have you noticed that in recent years, the colors of Christmas have expanded? They have taken on more of a home décor feel, and I decided to embrace it last year! In fact, for the first time ever, I put up a black Christmas tree and decorated it with black and white ornaments and white lights for a festive farmhouse feel. It was quite a departure from the traditional Christmas tree, but it turned out really lovely! (And it matched my house.)

Still, there's something magical about the true colors of Christmas—the rich reds, deep greens, royal purples, the elegant white, silver and golds, and the happy multi-colored lights. Did you know that your favorite Christmas color says something about your personality? Let me steal a line from Buddy in one of my favorite holiday movies, *Elf*. Remember the scene when he lunges over his father and answers the office phone: "Buddy the Elf, what's your favorite color?"

So…what's your favorite color of Christmas?

 If **RED** is your favorite color, various studies suggest that you are warm and cheery and love life. You are determined in your endeavors, dramatic and bright. Red is also the color of love and joy, which seems quite appropriate since it's one of the main colors of the Christmas color scheme, right? So why not be "the red" in somebody's

life this Christmas? Be the good cheer, warmth, and love to somebody. How, you ask? Well, you could be somebody's secret Santa. You know, surprise a depressed coworker with little fun gifts throughout the holiday season. Not to be recognized for your good deeds—just to do something unselfish and sweet for someone who needs a boost of joy this holiday season. Or watch your frazzled neighbor's kids so she can finish her Christmas shopping. Or drop in with a holiday basket of goodies and visit with that sweet woman who will be spending her first Christmas without her spouse. Just "be the red" in someone's life.

If **GREEN** is your favorite color, you are caring, affectionate, emotional, and optimistic—someone who believes the best and looks toward the future with hope and confidence. The color green also represents fresh beginnings and new life, which explains why it's such an important part of Christmas. Hanging greenery everywhere and decorating with the color green reminds us that Jesus came to earth as a baby to give us a new beginning. A new life! Because He came to earth and died on a cross for our sins, we get to become new creatures in Christ Jesus (2 Corinthians 5:17).

Do you know someone who needs a new beginning? Why not share Jesus with that person this Christmas? Truly, there's no better time than the present. I fear that in a world where being politically correct or too worried that we might offend someone has become the norm, we have stopped sharing the good news of Jesus Christ. Is there any better gift we could give someone who doesn't know the new beginning that's available through Jesus Christ? So go ahead. Give that gift this year.

If you're someone who can't choose just one favorite color but prefer a **MULTI-COLORED** strand of lights, it's safe to say that you're a person who loves unity, togetherness, and most importantly, the love of your Heavenly Father. You know, this theory is well-supported in the Scriptures. When Joseph's father gave him the coat of many colors, it was a symbol of his infinite love. And when God sent a rainbow to cover the earth after the great flood, it was a promise of love to Noah and all generations to come—a promise and representation of our Heavenly Father's Love.

Christmas is a great time to share God's love with others. People seem more open to it during the holiday season. But let me ask you this—are you experiencing God's love? Sure, you may know ABOUT God's love, but I want you to experience Him as Abba Father, like a Daddy, this Christmas and forevermore. Take time this holiday season and meditate on scriptures about His love. Here's one to get you started: *"And I am convinced that nothing can ever separate us from God's love. Neither death nor life, neither angels nor demons, neither our fears for today nor our worries about tomorrow—not*

With families getting together during the holiday season, there are some topics of conversation that should be avoided to prevent any family fighting, such as: politics, sports rivalries, and...white or colored Christmas lights.

No matter which side of the great light debate you embrace, you should know that this debate has been going on for many years.

Thomas Edison is credited with being the first one to string white lights together back in 1880, but Edward Johnson, an associate of Edison's, was the first one to create a string of red, white, and blue bulbs and place that colorful strand on a tree.[3]

And so, the great light debate was born.

I am a white light kind of girl because those white bursts of light create a perfect backdrop for all other types of ornaments and adornments we place on our Christmas trees.

Which do you prefer?

even the powers of hell can separate us from God's love. No power in the sky above or in the earth below—indeed, nothing in all creation will ever be able to separate us from the love of God that is revealed in Christ Jesus our Lord" (Romans 8:38-39, NLT).

So no matter which color of Christmas you fancy, you can be the red in someone's life this season; you can celebrate green and share the new beginning in Christ Jesus with a hurting world; and you can embrace the rainbow of God's love and let it bubble out of you and onto everyone you encounter this season. Merry multi-colored Christmas to you!

Hearth to Heaven

"Father God, help me to share Your love with every person I encounter this holiday season, and help me to better understand Your great love for me. Thank You, Lord, for a new beginning through Your Son, Jesus. I love You. Amen."

A GIFT FROM GOD

"My command is this: Love each other as I have loved you."

JOHN 15:12, NIV

Overflowing with Goodness

By Andy Clapp

We blast down the stairs, and then turn to see the bulging stockings hanging by the fireplace in the living room.

In the 1980s, the classic red and white stockings appeared in most homes. Our traditional stockings, complete with our names in glitter glue atop, held the sugary nectar we longed to enjoy. My sister and I dumped the contents onto the floor. We tore through the pile to find our favorite pieces.

For me, the chocolate coins wrapped in gold foil beckoned me to indulge. Small surprises hidden within the stocking heightened the moment.

Every year, hanging those stockings highlighted the day of decorating. Though they were empty when we hung them, we knew they would be full come Christmas morning.

Hung by the chimney, what stands empty on Christmas Eve overflows the next morning. Stockings accent the decorations of the season. Some choose the classic red felt stockings with white tops. Others hang more decorative stockings with snowmen or reindeer.

Families throughout history have had personal meanings behind why they put up stockings. Deeper in history, many nailed the stockings to the mantle. Others chose to hang the stockings from the tongs of the screen in front of the fireplace.

Both options kept the stockings in place. Now stocking holders add an extra layer of decoration to the mantle while accomplishing the same task as their wizened ancestors.

The tradition of stockings dates back to the days of Saint Nicholas. Legend tells that while passing through town, Nicholas overheard people discussing the distress of a local man. Afraid his poverty might affect his daughter's prospects of marriage, the father fretted about their future. Nicholas allegedly put gold in their stockings drying by the fireplace. The next morning, the girl found the blessing.

For those who never heard the legend, the importance of stockings stems from their inclusion in the poem "A Visit from Saint Nicholas." After Clement Clarke Moore wrote the iconic poem in 1823 the tradition became cemented in Christmas festivities. From their position by the fireplace, the stockings were filled by Santa on his journey around the world. Toys, candy, fruits, and nuts awaited the children when the new day dawned.

Reflecting on the scope of the impact stockings have on Christmas, companies now produce items to fit inside. "Stocking stuffers" increase the "wow" factor of a stocking on Christmas morning. Gift cards, small bottles of lotion or perfume, earrings, and small tools make the surprise even bigger for adults.

Millions of coloring pages depict stockings each Christmas. Featured in every holiday movie, the enduring image helps the heart to feel the warmth of Christmas. The hopes of children mirror the hopes of humanity as that which was empty will soon be filled. What once held nothing eventually overflows.

One lady experienced such a moment in her life. As she approached a well, there sat Jesus. They spoke, and Jesus promised, *"But whoever drinks from the water that I will give him will never get thirsty again—ever! In fact, the water I will give him will become a well of water springing up within him for eternal life"* (John 4:14, HCSB).

Her life before that moment matched that of a stocking on the day it is hung. Empty. Plenty of room for something but holding nothing. Relationships had drained her dry. Guilt deflated her hopes for a new life.

Then, she met the One who could fill her life like never before! A well of hope arose in that short interaction with Jesus.

Life tends to empty our lives. We run dry after seasons of running too hard. Stress robs us of any joy we once held. Arguments, disagreements, worries, and struggles siphon away the excitement that marked our lives just days before.

What fills your life this Christmas? Where do you turn for what you need each day?

There is hope for fulfillment that is more certain than hanging a stocking at Christmas. What Jesus offers is a guarantee, an assurance for the soul.

No longer does life have to feel empty. The search for fulfillment ends when we look to the Baby born in Bethlehem. Jesus promises to lead us to a life that overflows.

A recent study revealed that ninety-four percent of families hang stockings. The average amount spent filling each child's stocking is $10-25 in a majority of houses. Some of the most common stocking stuffers for men include small bottles of cologne, pocketknives, flashlights, money clips, and portable phone chargers. For women, common items are winter socks, jewelry, make-up, candles, and reusable straws.[4]

FESTIVE FUN FACTS

Remember this as you hang that stocking this year. Though you may feel empty at times, the promise of the Lord is to fill you up so that your life overflows. Turn to Him in expectation. Believe that He is able. Watch as He blesses you and His Spirit flows out of your life throughout the year.

The stockings will eventually be emptied out and put away until next year. But the fulfillment offered to our lives today does not run out. A life of abundance, as Jesus called it, awaits us. A cup that overflows, as David mentioned in Psalms 23, is within reach this Christmas for each of us.

Hearth to Heaven

"Dear Heavenly Father, we thank You today that our lives overflow. Your goodness and Your kindness fill up our lives every day of the year. Let us turn to You when we feel emptied out. Let your goodness overflow from our lives to the lives of those we come into contact with each day."

A GIFT FROM GOD

"You prepare a table before me in the presence of my enemies;
You anoint my head with oil; my cup overflows."

PSALMS 23:5, CSB

Give Yourself a Gift

By Michelle Medlock Adams

I love Christmas shopping. I make it my mission to find the perfect gift for every person on my list. In fact, if this writing thing ever goes south, I'm pretty sure I can make it as a personal shopper. I'm that good. But you know what I discovered a few years ago? One of the best gifts you can give (and receive) doesn't cost a penny. You can't find it in a store. And yet, it's the kind of gift that can change someone's life—including your own.

I'm talking about the gift of forgiveness. If you've been holding a grudge against someone, this is the perfect time to let it go, and forgive that person once and for all. Maybe you thought you'd forgiven that family member, but then you saw her at Thanksgiving, and you experienced that little tinge of "ickiness" in your heart. Or you're still harboring hurt in your heart toward that cantankerous co-worker who threw you under the bus at last month's meeting—let it go. Or you bumped into that former friend at a mutual friend's holiday party, and it literally took your breath away, and not in a good way. Forgive that former friend for your own sake! Wouldn't you love to get rid of those icky feelings? Wouldn't you love to live free from the hurt that's been plaguing your heart for far too long?

Well, you can if you are willing to offer forgiveness. You might say, "But, Michelle, that person isn't even sorry!" That's okay. That person doesn't have to be sorry in order for you to forgive. In fact, that person doesn't even have to be alive for you to offer forgiveness. If you're still harboring hurt over harsh words your late mother said to you, or if you're still suffering in your soul from abuse you experienced in a failed marriage, and that abuser has already passed on, it's time to choose forgiveness. Some grief experts even suggest writing a letter to that person, saying everything you always wanted to say but never had the opportunity to share, reading it out loud, writing "I forgive you" over the top of your letter in bold letters, and then shredding it or burning it. While that might seem pointless to you, it's not. It's an act of faith and a step toward the restoration of your heart. You don't have to feel it—just forgive by faith. God will help you. You see, forgiving someone doesn't mean you're condoning his or her inexcusable behavior; it just means that you're courageous enough to forgive and move forward.

I get it. Sometimes those hurts run so deep that you can't fathom ever forgiving the person who wronged you. But until you do, you'll never experience the freedom, peace,

and joy that God has for you. You ever heard the old saying, "Harboring unforgiveness in your heart is like drinking poison and expecting the other person to die"?

You're literally poisoning your heart and your life, and the person you're so upset with may not even know about your hurt. So, let it go.

Say it out loud right now—"Let it go!"

Lastly, you may be reading over this particular entry and thinking, "Well, this isn't for me. I don't need to forgive anyone. My heart is clean…" But is it? Sometimes, we don't need to forgive others; we need to forgive ourselves. Are you a prisoner of your own unforgiveness? Listen, if you've asked Jesus to forgive you, then it's already done. If God has forgiven you, why can't you forgive yourself? Do it by faith today. Forgive yourself and experience the gift of forgiveness, and all that goes with it—freedom, love, joy, peace, and more! I hope you'll let Jesus fill your heart today so that there is no room in there for any hurt. And I hope that you'll have the merriest Christmas Season ever.

Hearth to Heaven

"Father God, help me to give the gift of forgiveness to others, and help me to forgive myself, too. Thank You for forgiving me, even though I didn't deserve your mercy and grace. I'm so grateful for your forgiveness, Lord. I love You. Amen."

A GIFT FROM GOD

"Be kind and compassionate to one another, forgiving each other,
just as in Christ God forgave you"

EPHESIANS 4:32, NIV

Home Alone is one of the most famous and beloved holiday movies of all time. When people binge watch Christmas movies, *Home Alone* is always in that lineup. I understand why, too, because it's one of my favorites. It's funny, sweet, action-packed, and full of life lessons. I especially like the scene in the church. Remember that one? Old Man Marley, the scary next-door neighbor, sits next to Kevin and starts a conversation. After telling Kevin not to believe everything he hears, and that he didn't need to be afraid, Marley opens up about a family situation.

"I came to hear my granddaughter sing...I can't come hear her tonight," Marley says.

"You have plans?" Kevin asks.

"No, I'm not welcome," Marley answers, and he goes on to explain that his son doesn't want him around. "Years back, before you and your family moved on the block, I had an argument with my son...We lost our tempers, and I said I didn't care to see him anymore. He said the same, and we haven't spoken to each other since."

"If you miss him, why don't you call him?" Kevin asks.

Marley says that he is afraid that his son won't talk to him, and Kevin encourages him to call his son anyway.

"At least you'll know," Kevin says. "Then you could stop worrying about it. Then you won't have to be afraid anymore. I don't care how mad I was, I'd talk to my dad. Especially around the holidays."[5]

Then, on Christmas Day, we see Kevin looking out his window, and there is Marley, hugging his son. It's a beautiful scene of forgiveness. I cry every single time when it gets to that part of the movie. Maybe I am so moved because I'm praying for restoration in certain relationships in my life...just like Old Man Marley.

Well, why just watch it in the movies when you can experience it in your real life? I agree with Kevin...people are more apt to forgive and make up during the holiday season. So go ahead. Make the call. Write the note. Make the effort! And create your real life happy ending this year! C'mon. Let's do it together.

Day 7

The Guidance of God

By Andy Clapp

What drew the Wise Men garners the attention of people even today.

A star hangs in churches throughout the world. Smaller, illuminated stars hang from streetlamps. Star-shaped cookies sit ready to eat at gatherings throughout the season; some are even left for a special visitor on Christmas Eve. Families place a star at the top of the tree where the height leads everyone to look up and see. A Christmas Star announces the Christmas season as it shines bright for all to see.

Each year, we embark on a journey at our church. Cars gather in the parking lot, forming a single file line. My cousin stations himself in the back of his truck, holding a pole with an illuminated star. The pole extends five feet high, making sure all can see. His wife, Kelli, drives the truck for others to follow, a procession that leads through the streets of our little town of Liberty. The caravan ends at Brian and Kristyn Lowe's farm just outside the town.

In December 2018, the event fell on the eve of a major snowstorm. Though the ground was clear the Saturday night the event was held, a foot of snow blanketed the area the next day. The temperatures plummeted throughout the day and at the end of the journey, Cliff hustled to the burn barrels.

"How bad was the drive?" I asked.

He cracked his grin, then assured me, "It was a little chilly." He rubbed his hands as he stood as close to the barrel as humanly possible.

As a flood of people emerged from their cars, we gathered outside the live nativity. They followed the star to the place where they would hear about Jesus.

The event harkens back to the star of Bethlehem two-thousand years ago. God provided for the Wise Men and guided them to the exact place they needed to go. Matthew wrote, *"It led them until it came and stopped above the place where the child was"* (Matthew 2:9b, HCSB). At the end of the journey, they saw what life is all about.

No need to search any further. They traversed hundreds of miles and then came to the place where they found Jesus. The star's guidance wasn't to a general location. God assured their journey culminated with His purpose. They stood before the One, the fulfillment of the promise of God.

How is God leading you this Christmas? Do you see His hand in your life as He leads you to where He wants you to be? God never stops guiding His people. One assurance we have is that He always leads us to a place that is closer to Him! He promises us that if we follow Him, our destination will be where we are meant to be.

Are your eyes open this year? So many missed the very star the Wise Men followed. For hundreds of years, they were told He was coming. A huge star announced He was here. But so many missed what God placed in front of their very eyes. This year,

In December of 2020, Jupiter and Saturn aligned so close that they appeared like the Star of Bethlehem. According to Popsugar, the phenomenon had not been witnessed in nearly eight-hundred years. To have seen a closer alignment of the planets, you would have to go back to March of 1226.[6]

let's open our eyes to see where He is leading us today. Let's tune our hearts to be led by the Lord.

Don't be like the masses who reach the end of life only to realize they missed the mark. He's leading you to Jesus this Christmas. You may have to endure some cold, some distance, and some obstacles, but at the end, the journey is worth it.

Hearth to Heaven

"Dear Heavenly Father, lead us back to the place where our hearts and souls call home. Open our eyes to see where You want us to be. Lead us closer to Jesus this Christmas. Take us back to the heart of Christmas and define our Christmas by our worship above all else. We commit to following wherever You lead because we know that at the end, we will see Jesus. In Jesus' name we pray, Amen."

A GIFT FROM GOD

"After hearing the king, they went on their way. And there it was—
the star they had seen in the east! It led them until it came and stopped
above the place where the child was."

MATTHEW 2:9, HCSB

Day 8

The Charlie Brown Christmas Tree

By Michelle Medlock Adams

I love Christmas trees. All kinds. Artificial ones. Real ones. Small ones. Big ones. Elaborately adorned ones. Simply decorated ones. I love them all! I have always been especially fond of the pitiful little tree in that famous animated holiday special, *A Charlie Brown Christmas.*[7]

Remember that one? Lucy tells Charlie Brown to pick out a great big aluminum Christmas tree, maybe a pink one, for the Christmas play. So Charlie Brown and Linus head to the local Christmas tree lot, but they pass by all of the colorful aluminum trees and walk right over to a little pine tree on a sad, wooden stand.

"This little green one seems to need a home," Charlie Brown says.

"I don't know, Charlie Brown. Remember what Lucy said? This doesn't seem to fit the modern spirit," Linus answers.

"I don't care. We'll decorate it and it will be just right for our play. Besides, I think it needs me." Charlie Brown picks up the tiny tree. Most of its needles fall to the ground. When they return to the auditorium, Charlie Brown places it on top of Schroeder's piano. The kids all gather round and ridicule Charlie Brown and his poor little tree.

"You were supposed to get a good tree," Lucy yells. "Can't you even tell a good tree from a poor tree?"

The laughing and mean remarks continue until everyone leaves except Linus.

"I guess you were right, Linus," Charlie Brown says. "I shouldn't have picked this little tree. Everything I do turns into a disaster. I guess I really don't know what Christmas is all about. Isn't there anyone who knows what Christmas is all about?"

Then Linus answers with a reading from the Gospel of Luke, Chapter 2:8-14 (KJV). Although the version below is slightly different than what appears in the film, this is quoted from the King James Version: *"And there were in the same country shepherds abiding in the field, keeping watch over their flock by night. And, lo, the angel of the Lord came upon them, and the glory of the Lord shown round about them: and they were sore afraid. And the angel said unto them, Fear not, for, behold, I bring you good tidings of great joy, which shall be to all people. For unto you is born this day in the city of David a Saviour, which is Christ the Lord. And this shall be a sign unto you; Ye shall find the babe wrapped in swaddling clothes, lying in a manger. And suddenly there was with the angel a multitude of the heavenly host praising God, and saying, 'Glory to God in the highest, and on earth peace, good will toward men.'"*

"That's what Christmas is all about, Charlie Brown," Linus gently shares.

So Charlie Brown takes the sad little tree home and decides to decorate it, but the sparse tiny tree is so frail that one little ornament bends it completely over. Charlie Brown thinks he has killed the tree and leaves in disgust. Soon, the other kids gather around the tree. Linus straightens the bent branch and carefully wraps his blanket around the base of the tree.

"It's not bad at all, really," Linus says. "Maybe it just needs a little love."[8]

The kids take decorations from Snoopy's doghouse and place them on Charlie Brown's tree. Suddenly, the little tree is transformed!

The late, great Charles Schulz certainly packed a powerful message into such a scrawny tree story, didn't he? Each year when this beloved Christmas special airs, it reminds us that Jesus is the real reason for the season, causing us to take our focus off the glitz and commercialism of Christmas, and refocus our eyes on the beautiful message of the Manger.

Maybe you needed that reminder today, that Jesus is the reason for the season. Or maybe you feel a lot like that sad, little tree—standing all alone in that Christmas tree lot. The holidays can feel awfully lonely. Or maybe, like that little tree, you've been ridiculed and overlooked. Or maybe you've never felt very special or loved. If that's you, hold on! Have I got good news for you! In the same way that Linus wrapped his blanket around the base of that pitiful little pine tree, Jesus is wrapping his massive arms of love around you today (Psalms 91:4, TPT)! He wants you to know that He will never leave you or forsake you, so you're not alone in this world (Deuteronomy 31:6). And He wants you to know that He took special care creating you. He made you on purpose for a purpose (Psalms 139:13-16).

I hope you never look at a Christmas tree the same way again. Let it be a reminder of just how special this Christmas season really is, and just how precious you truly are to God. Merry Christmas.

Hearth to Heaven

"Father God, thank You for sending Your Son so that I could be saved. And thank You for loving me and promising to never leave me. Help me, Lord, to see myself in Your eyes and understand how special I am to You. Amen."

A GIFT FROM GOD

"But you are not like that, for you are a chosen people. You are royal priests,[a] a holy nation, God's very own possession. As a result, you can show others the goodness of God, for he called you out of the darkness into his wonderful light."

1 PETER 2:9, NLT

Sometimes the story behind the story is just as good as the actual story! That's the case when it comes to *A Charlie Brown Christmas*.

According to an article that appeared in the December 8, 2021 issue of *Newsweek*, the thirty-minute animated Christmas special wasn't birthed through creativity, but rather through obligation. It was sort of commissioned by a commercial sponsor who saw merit in turning the country's favorite newspaper cartoon into an animated TV special. As Lee Mendelson, the person who eventually produced *A Charlie Brown Christmas*, described it: "We got a call from Coca-Cola...and they said, 'Have you and Mr. Schulz ever considered doing a Charlie Brown show?' And I lied, and said, 'Absolutely, we've been thinking about it.' And this was on a Thursday. And they said, 'We have to make a decision on Monday. Can you send us an outline of the show?'"

That phone conversation led to another one—this one was with Mr. Schulz. Mendelson told him what had just transpired, summing it up like this: "I have good news and bad news. The good news is I think I just sold *A Charlie Brown Christmas*. The bad news is we have to write it tomorrow."

So they went to work, made the sale, and the rest is history.[9]

A Light in the Darkness

By Andy Clapp

A light pierces the darkness of a winter's night.

In each window of houses and churches, a candle stands centered and illuminated. Four candles circle an advent wreath with a larger candle in the middle. Carolers clutch candles as they sing of the joy of the season.

The tradition of candles dates back to the Middle Ages. Today, candles accent the landscape far and wide when Christmas comes around. A candle represents the Star of Bethlehem.

The mention of candles takes me straight back to memories of Christmas candlelight services at our church. My first Christmas as a pastor, I anxiously approached the service where lights shone in the beautiful sanctuary of a nearly two-hundred-year-old church. In my excitement, I forgot to calculate in how long the candles would burn according to my order of service.

I preached my heart out. Tied in was nearly every reference to light in the Bible. At the end, the majesty of a Baptist church singing "Silent Night" filled the air. I assured myself it had been the greatest candlelight service ever conducted.

The next morning, however, I woke up to an email:

"Hot wax drips onto trousers when candles stay lit so long."

Panic ran through my soul. I rushed to the church to see if a mess remained after what had been a beautiful service.

Sure enough, circles of wax dotted the pews and the floor. The custodians faced quite the job as roughly a hundred candles left trails in the sanctuary.

Graciously, the custodians smiled. "The service was beautiful. We can get this cleaned up."

I jumped in to help remove the hardened wax. By the end of the day, all was well. No wax remained. Though I remember the mess, I remember the peace of the service even more. With all the lights cut down, the lighting of each candle provided enough light to overcome the darkness.

Amazing to me is the sense of peace found in the small flame of a candle. Whether it be one candle or a hundred, the presence of a candle's light gives a flicker of hope, a calming assurance in the depth of the night that everything will be all right.

Jesus pierced the darkness of the world when He was born in Bethlehem. Like a small flame flickering in the night, the stable held the light of the world. Though multitudes of attempts have been made to extinguish His light, it continues to shine today. As John so poignantly recorded, *"That light shines in the darkness, yet the darkness did not overcome it"* (John 1:5, HCSB). A simple stable held the world's brightest light that night in Bethlehem.

Though the world seemed to miss it, the candle lit in Bethlehem continued to burn beyond a single era. The darkness of sin held no power over the light of Christ. A Savior is born—a light gives birth to hope for all people.

What a few saw in Bethlehem, masses saw later. In Him, they witnessed something different from the world. The darkened days of before held less power after the night

He came to Bethlehem. A pure light shone from a barn of all places, a light not for a moment, but for eternity.

You look at your own life and wonder if it matters. You see yourself as just one of billions, but a single candle makes a difference. A single light inspires others to break from the darkness. One life illuminated by the Lord shines the way to new life for others.

See your life this season and beyond as a candle. A single candle can break even the deepest, most expansive darkness. You may be the one light in someone's life that points them to Jesus. You can be the light in your home, your school, in your workplace, and in your community that shines so brightly it cannot be ignored.

This world needs light. As you burn for Jesus, others can see the light of truth. The darkness did not overcome the light of Jesus. In the same way, the darkness will not be able to overcome the light of Jesus in your life if you commit to being a candle in this world of darkness.

Most of us need a boost of boldness to continue shining for the Lord in these times.

Let's be the ones who refuse to blend in with the darkness. Let's shine for Jesus every day!

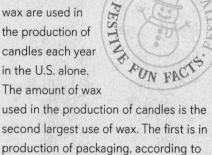

More than one billion pounds of wax are used in the production of candles each year in the U.S. alone. The amount of wax used in the production of candles is the second largest use of wax. The first is in production of packaging, according to candles.org.[10]

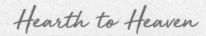

Hearth to Heaven

"Dear Lord, I want to be a candle for You in this world full of darkness. Give me the boldness I need to shine for You, not just in this season, but for the rest of my days. Give me a passion for You that burns so brightly that others take note. In Jesus' name I pray, Amen."

A Gift from God

"That light shines in the darkness, yet the darkness did not overcome it."

JOHN 1:5, HCSB

Message in an Ornament

By Michelle Medlock Adams

I couldn't wait to decorate our Christmas tree that year. As Jeff wrapped the lights around the branches, I unwrapped each ornament that we'd carefully stored the year before. Well, I *thought* we had carefully stored them, but as it turned out, I hadn't wrapped all of the breakable ones in enough bubble wrap and tissue paper because a few of them were broken, including my red glittery "Peace" ornament. Instead of saying, "Peace," it said, "Pea."

I mean, I don't even like peas.

Not exactly the same sentiment…

However, we had a good laugh about it and retired that ornament.

So I haven't had "Peace" on my tree since that Christmas, but I still have peace in my heart. I hope you do too.

You know, there's a lot of talk about peace during the Christmas season. Some of us decorate our trees with it. We send out holiday cards that say, "Peace to your family." And we sing Christmas carols with lyrics like, "Peace on earth." You might say that peace is "trending" this time of year, but as Christians we don't have to wait until the Christmas season to enjoy it. In fact, if we ask Jesus into our lives, we can experience peace all year through.

Not the superficial, glittery kind that can be broken. God's kind of peace isn't a temporal thing that is affected by the outside world or negative circumstances. It's a peace that passes all understanding.

John 14:27 (NIV) says, *"Peace I leave with you; my peace I give you. I do not give to you as the world gives. Do not let your hearts be troubled and do not be afraid."*

Life can get crazy, especially this time of year, and if you're experiencing an overly busy schedule, stressful family get-togethers, financial challenges, illness, or any other kind of struggle, you're not alone (even if you feel like you are). As a Christian, Jesus is always with you. He promises to never leave you or forsake you. And Jesus is the Prince of Peace. If He resides in your heart, then peace also lives there.

So I say, Merry Christmas and Peace be with you this season and all year through.

In case you're searching for peace, and not the glittery ornament kind, here are ten scriptures to meditate on and possibly memorize this Christmas season.

1 *"Now may the Lord of peace himself give you his peace at all times and in every situation. The Lord be with you all."* –2 Thessalonians 3:16, NLT

2   *"For God is not a God of disorder but of peace."*
    –1 Corinthians 14:33a, NLT

3   *"You will keep in perfect peace all who trust in you, all whose*
    thoughts are fixed on you!" –Isaiah 26:3, NLT

4   *"In peace I will lie down and sleep, for you alone, O Lord, will keep*
    me safe." –Psalms 4:8, NLT

5   *"Lord, you will grant us peace; all we have accomplished is really*
    from you." –Isaiah 26:12, NLT

6   *"Great peace have those who love your law, and nothing can make*
    them stumble." –Psalms 119:165, NIV

7   *"The fruit of that righteousness will be peace; its effect will be*
    quietness and confidence forever" –Isaiah 32:17, NIV

8   *"You will go out in joy and be led forth in peace; the mountains and*
    hills will burst into song before you, and all the trees of the field
    will clap their hands." –Isaiah 55:12, NIV

9   *"Mercy, peace and love be yours in abundance."*
    –Jude 1:2, NIV

10 *"May the God of hope fill you with all joy and peace as you trust*
    in him, so that you may overflow with hope by the power of the
    Holy Spirit." –Romans 15:13, NIV

Hearth to Heaven

"Dear God, in the midst of this chaotic world, I'm asking that You fill me with Your supernatural peace. I love You. Amen."

A GIFT FROM GOD

"For to us a child is born, to us a son is given, and the government will be on his shoulders. And he will be called Wonderful Counselor, Mighty God, Everlasting Father, Prince of Peace."

ISAIAH 9:6, NIV

A Gift a Day

By Andy Clapp

Each day, a treasure awaits.

Children and adults enjoy the Advent calendar. As they count down the days until Christmas morning, each day provides a little blessing. Many choose the calendars with pieces of chocolate.

I never knew what Advent calendars were until my first Christmas with my wife. The tradition was a part of her family's celebration, so we set out to find these calendars to incorporate into our own festivities.

"But we already have a calendar hanging on the wall," I explained, believing this to be a piece of paper to mark off the days.

"It's not the same thing," she said.

I tried to process her words. My understanding hung on the word "calendar."

"Each day, you open it up and get a piece of chocolate out of the calendar," she further explained.

"Chocolate?"

"Yes, honey. There is a piece of chocolate for every day."

My aggravation immediately gave way to jubilation. "All right! Where do you buy these things?"

She laughed at the dramatic shift that occurred once I realized chocolate was involved.

Every year since, Advent calendars are the second purchase of the Christmas season. First, we get the tree. Second, we buy the chocolate. Of all our traditions, this stands as one of our children's favorites, one we passed on to them as soon as they could eat chocolate.

A blessing each day stands just a door of the calendar away.

Christmas is such a blessed season. From the time with friends and family, to the exchanging of gifts, blessings abound at Christmas. The greatest of all the blessings is the coming of the Son of God into the world.

God used prophets to tell of the coming of the Son. He gave desperate people something grand to look forward to. The Wise Men were able to see Jesus because they waited in eager anticipation. Just by the words they spoke, we understand their attentiveness to the time.

They kept a trained eye on the sky. As they entered Jerusalem, they proclaimed, *"For we saw His star in the east and have come to worship Him"* (Matthew 2:2b, HCSB). So filled with anticipation were these foreign kings that they moved when the star appeared. They saw the star because they waited for the moment. When it came, they travelled eagerly to where He was.

Why did others miss such a sign? How is it that the world missed out even with such a

FESTIVE FUN FACTS · FESTIVE FUN FACTS ·

Advent calendars feature various treats for each day of the first twenty-four days of December. Some have chocolate for each day, while others have Legos, samples of beauty products, and even tea and coffee samples. According to the New York Post, the most expensive Advent Calendar cost over ten million dollars. Designed by Debbie Wingham, the calendar featured watches and even diamonds.[11]

noticeable star in the sky? For the Wise Men, they longed for the moment of the star's appearance. They studied. They watched. They waited. Each passing day led to greater excitement as they inched closer to the big day.

Advent calendars breed excitement and anticipation. Each day, a small chocolate blessing awaits and each day, anticipation rises as the big day, Christmas Day, draws nearer. Yet the anticipation and eagerness have no reason to escape after Christmas Day. There is more to be excited and watchful for throughout the year.

He's coming again! Just as the Wise Men kept an eye of anticipation toward the sky when He came to Bethlehem, we eagerly await the signs for His coming a second time. The wisest among us see the blessing each day brings while rejoicing as each day brings us one day closer.

Are you eager in anticipation for Christmas? We all are. We cannot wait to celebrate. The same level of joy, excitement, and readiness should mark each day in every season as we wait for Him to return to earth once more.

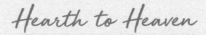

Hearth to Heaven

"Heavenly Father, thank You for the little blessings that each day brings. As we eagerly await Christmas Day's arrival, let us live with an eagerness about Jesus coming every day. May we praise You each day as we come closer to seeing Jesus again. In Jesus' name we pray, Amen."

A GIFT FROM GOD

"Then we who are still alive will be caught up together with them in the clouds to meet the Lord in the air and so we will always be with the Lord. Therefore encourage one another with these words."

1 THESSALONIANS 4:17-18, HCSB

The Grief That Stole Christmas

By Michelle Medlock Adams

Not all Christmas movies are created equal. While most Christmas movies are full of cheesy cheer and warm wishes, sprinkled with snow flurries and giddy wonderment, some are a little more realistic and…sad.

I made the mistake of watching one of those tearjerker Christmas flicks last year. The movie? *The Family Stone*. Now I'm not saying it's not a good movie, because I love Diane Keaton and Sarah Jessica Parker, but geez! So sad! *The Family Stone* is not a new movie. In fact, it released in 2005, I had just never watched it until last year. But if you're binging holiday movies throughout November and December, *The Family Stone* is bound to show up as a choice on one of your movie channels. Spoiler alert—the matriarch of the fam, Diane Keaton, shares that she has a terminal illness and that this will most likely be her last Christmas. (Did I mention I cried for an hour after the credits rolled?)

Of course, it might be that this particular movie hit a little too close to home because my sweet mama died of cancer in May 2006, and those memories of our first Christmas without her came rushing back. I still remember that year like it was yesterday. I stumbled through Mother's Day, her birthday, and the summer months, still numb from her passing, but I dreaded that first holiday season. Thanksgiving had been hard enough—I just couldn't bear facing the empty chair at Christmas. That was Mom's favorite holiday, and she did it up big every year. She was truly the Queen of Christmas, and I just couldn't imagine Christmas without her.

When I phoned my older sister to tell her we wouldn't be home for the holidays, she was devastated.

"But we need each other, especially this year," she cried. "Please come home."

I know it might have been selfish, but I just couldn't go through the motions that year. My husband and I and our two daughters headed to Hollywood Beach, Florida, for a totally non-traditional Christmas. We didn't even put up a Christmas tree at home.

Instead, we packed our bathing suits and spent Christmas morning on the beach—no present opening, no Christmas cookies, just us, God, and the ocean.

We were in survival mode, and that's how we survived our first Christmas without Mom. The four of us bonded in a new way and remembered her as we walked along the beach at sunset Christmas night. I also spent some time by myself, sitting on the beach, crying out to God, being honest with Him about my disappointment, and allowing Him to love on me in a way I'd never experienced before. It was a very non-traditional Christmas, but it was very sweet and meaningful, and it was exactly what we needed.

Maybe you're going through your first holiday season without a loved one, and if you are, I get it. I feel your pain. I'm not a certified grief counselor, so I can't tell you how to get through your grief, but I can tell you this—you're not alone on this grief journey. Your Heavenly Father promises that He will never leave you or forsake you. And He also promises to comfort you. 2 Corinthians 1:3 (TPT) says, *"All praises belong to the God and Father of our Lord Jesus Christ. For he is the Father of tender mercy and the God of endless comfort."*

Endless comfort—isn't that wonderful?

There are some practical things you can do, of course, to help you get through this holiday season if you're experiencing grief. Make sure you get enough rest. Eat nutritious meals. Work in workouts on a regular basis. Don't allow yourself to be isolated. Spend time in the Word and in God's presence every day. And take time to praise God every morning. If you do all of these things, am I saying you won't suffer from grief this holiday season? No, but I am saying that doing those things will help you find the beauty of this season despite the loss you're feeling. Oh, and let me add one more bit of advice. Don't watch sad Christmas movies, whether it's your first holiday season without your loved one, or your sixteenth—why open that door to grief? Instead, make Christmas cookies with your children or go caroling with a group from church. Fill your time with happy activities and make new, joyful memories.

One thing I've discovered about grief is this—sometimes it sneaks up on you. And I think that's even more true during the holiday season. You're fine one minute, and then you run into the store to pick up gift bags, and someone passes you wearing the same perfume that your loved one always wore. Then, whoosh! That wave of grief smacks you right in the face, and the tears begin to flow. And that's okay. Give yourself permission to grieve; just don't let the grief overtake your life and keep you from truly living.

I was watching a TV show the other night and one of the characters said: "Grief doesn't ever get lighter. We just get used to carrying the weight."[12] While that makes for great dialogue in a television drama, it's certainly not an accurate statement. You see, as Christians, we were never meant to carry that weight. So if you're feeling tired today from carrying the weight of grief, give it to God. He will carry the grief, and He will carry you.

Hearth to Heaven

"Father God, thank You for loving me through this loss. Help me, Lord, to never lose sight of You and the fact that Your promises are still true, despite my disappointment. I am grateful that You promise to never leave me, and I'm so thankful that Your comfort is endless. I give this holiday season to You. Please bless it, Lord. Amen."

A GIFT FROM GOD

"The Lord is close to the brokenhearted and saves those who are crushed in spirit."

PSALMS 34:18, NIV

FESTIVE FOCUS · FESTIVE FOCUS ·

Maybe you aren't experiencing grief this Christmas, but you know people who are facing their first holiday season without a loved one. Why not reach out to that family in love?

Here are three tangible ways you can make a difference and be the hands and feet of Jesus this Christmas.

Listen: Let that grieving family share memories of the loved one who has passed on. Just listen. The act of listening is such a loving gesture.

Ask: Rather than asking, "Is there anything I can do for you?" to that grieving family, be more specific. For example, ask: "Could I get groceries for you?" Or, "Could I run some errands for you?" If you see a need, simply ask if you can fill it.

Offer: Why not offer to do something to honor their loved one? Like planting a tree or making a charitable donation or releasing a sky lantern. Look for unique ways to remember their loved one.

It's A Wonderful Life

By Andy Clapp

A black and white film whisks us back to a simpler time while teaching us a timeless truth.

The legendary film marks the Christmas season for a majority of people. Jimmy Stewart plays a role that we can identify with in our lives. What seems to be a series of broken dreams and other frustrations convince George Bailey (Stewart) that it would be better for all if he'd never been born. In utter despair, he is determined to end his life.

An angel gives him a chance to see what the town would be like if he'd never been born. Lives would be lost because he hadn't been in a place to save them. The fortunes of so many drastically changed when George was no longer a part of their lives' equations. He learned that his life held value and after his eyes were opened to a world without him, he longed to live again.

Troubles shrouded the blessing his life was until that blessing was taken away. As he exclaims near the end of the movie, "I want to live again!" he reveals the perspective that comes in the wake of losing everything.

It's easy for us to arrive at the same place as George Bailey, wishing we'd never drawn that first breath. Life features setbacks and a fair share of disappointments. We strive to do good but fail to see the results of those efforts. Bombarded by frustrations, we forget there is a meaning and a purpose to each of our lives.

We are needed. Our lives hold immense value. And Christmas proves it.

As Joseph laid down to rest, he needed a reprieve. Since Mary had told him the story of the angel's visit, his mind raced. So many questions arose. Yet, a decision still had to be made: What should he do with Mary and the unborn Child?

He decided to spare her life and the Child's, choosing instead to divorce her privately. It felt to be a righteous decision. His mind and heart calmed, and he laid down.

An interruption to his rest tells us of our lives' priceless nature. The angel told Joseph, *"She will give birth to a son, and you are to name Him Jesus, because He will save His people from their sins"* (Matthew 1:21, HCSB). Joseph listened. He followed the instructions of the angel, and we know how the story unfolds.

But do you see your value? Do you see that there is purpose in your days?

He came to save His people. He came to save each one of us because we are worth saving! Your life holds incredible value to the One who created you.

As we approach Christmas and the end of another year, we journey back to a stable in Bethlehem. Our eyes focus on the Son of God, born into a world that would reject Him. In that manger, we uncover the depth of value that we hold to God. He came for you. You are important enough that Jesus gave up heaven to walk the earth.

According to *Mental Floss*, the entire work of *It's A Wonderful Life* began as a Christmas card. The card made its way into the hands of a producer at RKO Pictures and from there, a tradition was born.[13]

Regardless of the disappointments of yesterday, God has a plan for you today. This season embrace the impact you have on others as you live a life of sacrifice. Though the world discounts you, Jesus chose to die for you.

Find the reason to live in the One who came to walk among us. Begin to see this as a wonderful life because in Jesus, this is truly a wonderful existence. The timeless truth of a film draws us to the reality that life is a gift given by the Author of life itself.

In this awesome season, see the beauty of this wonderful life!

Hearth to Heaven

"Dear Heavenly Father, open our eyes this Christmas to see the beauty of the life You've given to us. Let us live in the assurance that our lives hold meaning and purpose in You. Give us a passion to live and allow us to embrace the value You place in our lives. Thank You for loving us so much that You sent Jesus to the earth. In Jesus' name we pray, Amen."

A GIFT FROM GOD

"A thief comes only to steal and to kill and to destroy.
I have come so that they may have life and have it in abundance."

JOHN 10:10, CSB

Fruitcake, Anyone?

By Michelle Medlock Adams

Christmas and fruitcakes go hand in hand, although I've never met anyone who actually likes fruitcake…have you? There's a long-running joke that claims only one fruitcake truly exists in the world. It's just that it's never been eaten but rather it's been re-gifted thousands of times throughout history. Of course, you better not make that joke if you happen to be in Claxton, Georgia, or Corsicana, Texas. You see, both Claxton and Corsicana have proudly deemed their cities, "Fruitcake Capital of the World." Bakeries in those two towns start preparing for their fruitcake festivities as early as August, just to keep up with the orders. Who knew?[14]

Fruitcakes, as Christmas presents go, are probably never going to make one of those "Best Gift Ever!" lists, and that's okay. But have you ever tried a sliver of fruitcake? I remember one Christmas Eve when I was about twelve years old. The whole family had gathered at our house, including my mom's older sister, Aunt Muriel. I loved it when she visited because Aunt Muriel was an amazing cook, and her desserts were legendary. I remember helping her bring in all of her covered dishes, hoping she'd brought her famous fudge, and planning to steal a few pieces before anyone else could get their hands on it. I carefully removed the foil from a platter that I was sure showcased her creamy peanut butter fudge, so you can imagine my surprise when instead, I discovered…a fruitcake.

"I see you found my fruitcake," Aunt Muriel beamed. "Go ahead, dear, try it!"

Just as I was about to concoct a story about being allergic to fruitcake, Aunt Muriel acted with Ninja-like precision, slicing off a small sliver and shoving it into my mouth. Stunned, my first instinct was to spit it out, but the fruitcake's incredible flavor stopped me.

"This is actually good," I said, talking as I chewed.

"Well, of course it is," Aunt Muriel responded. "I made it."

I don't know if Aunt Muriel's fruitcake was the exception, or if I actually like all fruitcake, but I certainly liked her version. Granted, I've never tasted another crumb of fruitcake since that Christmas Eve, but at least I can say I've tried it, and I liked it. Now that doesn't mean I want you to re-gift all of your fruitcakes to me. And to be honest, I probably wouldn't ever give the gift of fruitcake because I like to give presents that might appear on the "Best Gift Ever" list.

You know what tops that list? Jesus!

He truly is the best gift ever, and He is totally re-giftable. You can share Jesus with everyone on your gift list. The world is desperate for hope, love, and peace. Jesus offers all of those things and more, but you know, the Good News only becomes "the Good News" when you choose to share it. So go ahead. Step outside your comfort zone this Christmas and share Jesus with your family and friends who might never have received the gift of salvation. Don't worry if they have rejected Him in the past. They may not have been ready to receive Him when you shared your testimony before. I find that often, people reject Jesus simply because of what they've heard Christianity is all about, when in fact, what they've heard is not an accurate portrayal of our Savior and His unconditional love. They just need to taste and see that the Lord is good…kind of like I needed to do with Aunt Muriel's fruitcake. Why not share the Best Gift Ever with someone today?

Hearth to Heaven

"Father God, help me to share the Good News with my friends and family this holiday season without fear of being rejected. Please open the door for me to share my testimony. Pave the way, Lord, so that I can share Your love with my loved ones. Amen."

A Gift from God

"Taste and see that the Lord is good; blessed is the one who takes refuge in him."

PSALMS 34:8, NIV

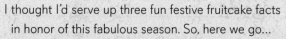

I thought I'd serve up three fun festive fruitcake facts in honor of this fabulous season. So, here we go...

Apparently, fruitcake really is forever. According to a column that appeared in a 1983 *New York Times* issue, a man named Russell Baker claimed to own a fruitcake that a past relative had baked in 1794 as a Christmas present for then-President George Washington. The myth states that Washington returned the fruitcake with an added note saying that it's "unseemly for Presidents to accept gifts weighing more than 80 pounds, even though they were only eight inches in diameter." But wait, the story gets even crazier! Apparently, Baker and his relatives gathered every year to carve off a tiny bit of the fruitcake to share...and yes, eat! Yuck!

A fruitcake—a pineapple one, to be exact—went to space on Apollo 11. However, no one on that mission consumed even a morsel of it while in space, so the intact fruitcake is on display at the Smithsonian Air and Space Museum in Washington, D.C.

Though most people loathe fruitcakes, that freaky little fruitcake has still managed to get its own month. As you might have guessed, December is National Fruitcake Month.[15]

Day 15

The Nutcracker

By Andy Clapp

For years, I saw the nutcrackers in stores but didn't know what they had to do with Christmas. Toy soldiers also kept me in suspense, their lighted displays catching my eye and eventually piquing my curiosity.

I knew of the ballet, but to be honest, I never thought more about it. Ballet wasn't quite my thing. But once I experienced the show myself, it was a time never to be forgotten.

Later in the days of September 2019, I heard a familiar sound in the air at my house. A tune, often identified with Christmas, played as my daughters listened.

"Do you know what music that is, Daddy?" my daughter asked.

"I sure do…but do you?" I responded, wanting to see if she had learned the material.

As part of their homeschool curriculum, they would learn about famous artists and composers. They'd spend time listening to classical music and then identify who composed the songs.

"Cha-something," she said as she looked her mother's way.

"Tchaikovsky," Crystal said.

"Yeah, that guy," she told me, proud she at least got the first syllable correct.

For Pyotr Ilyich Tchaikovsky, the composition became one of, if not the, most recognizable of his career. The very score replays year after year, a masterpiece to those who love *The Nutcracker* ballet so dearly. The score brings up Tchaikovsky's name every December even though he died in 1893. Audiences enjoy his work, the beauty of his composition ensuring the Russian composer stays at the front of people's minds.

These songs written to last have endured over a hundred and twenty-five years since he passed.

Such a score pulls us into the bigger story, chiming the steps of Claire, Fritz, Drosselmeyer, the Mouse King, and the Nutcracker.

Each Christmas, we focus on certain Bible passages. Isaiah and Micah point to the coming of Christ. Luke 1 reveals how Mary learned of her role and Luke 2:1-20 can be recited by nearly all who are lifelong churchgoers. But what's often missed is the beautiful song of Mary's soul, the soundtrack of someone in the heart of the unfolding events.

Mary's song is recorded late in Luke 1. Being chosen by God humbled her and overwhelmed her simultaneously. Of all the women in the world, God chose her for this cause—to give birth to the Savior of the world. Her song's inclusion in the Bible reveals God's value for the song of her heart in those moments. She praised God, who had sought to use her.

Her song reflects the greatness of God. The words demand our attention because we, too, need to rejoice. God is great. We have a Savior. He has looked on us with favor. Mary's song lives on because it is a proclamation of how great God is and the mighty work of His hand.

Bethlehem shows us the greatness of God. Christmas draws out of us a song of rejoicing for what He has done, what He is doing, and what He will do. Mary knew the specialness of the call of God on her life. He chose her. Just as her selection led her to praise, our selection should lead us to such a spirit. The melody of the heart every day, but especially here at Christmas, is one of joy and humility.

First, He stands as Savior. God sent Who we needed so that we could be set free through Jesus. Just that brings out a song in the soul of the redeemed.

> *The Nutcracker* ballet is one of the most well-known ballets in the world, alongside Swan Lake. The premiere of *The Nutcracker* in the U.S. took place in 1944, fifty-two years after its debut in St. Petersburg, Russia. The first performance in the United States was in San Francisco.[16]

Secondly, He calls to you and uses you. Mary felt unworthy but was willing. When she sang, she joyfully reflected on the Lord's decision to use her. Be filled with a song of joy as the Lord uses your life.

Some songs stand the test of time. Let your song of life be one that sings of a God who stands throughout time!

Hearth to Heaven

"Dear Lord, as Mary praised You that day, so we praise You today. Great and mighty are Your works. You amaze us each day. Thank You for salvation and grace. Thank You for choosing to use us while we are here on earth, May the song of our lives speak to Your greatness and carry on in the generations to come."

A GIFT FROM GOD

"But I will sing of Your strength and will joyfully proclaim
Your faithful love in the morning."

PSALMS 59:16, HCSB

Don't Let the Grinch Steal Your Christmas

By Michelle Medlock Adams

I've always loved the animated holiday special, "How the Grinch Stole Christmas!" You remember that famous story, right? The Grinch was not a fan of Christmas or anything that went along with it.

> *"The Grinch hated Christmas! The whole Christmas Season!*
> *Now, please don't ask why. No one quite knows the reason."* [17]

Well, I haven't seen the actual Grinch wandering the streets this holiday season, but I can tell you this—he's alive and active! And he is out to steal your Christmas! Now, he won't sneak in your house with his big old empty bag and fill it with your Christmas tree, your stockings, or even your "Who beast," but THIS Grinch will steal your contentment, your joy, and your peace.

And he goes by the name of…Stress.

Are you experiencing the "hustle and bustle" of the season? Is your December so jam-packed with events, holiday parties, and obligatory get-togethers that you are wondering when you'll have time to schedule a bathroom break? Are you feeling more stressed than blessed this time of year?

If so, the Grinch may have already paid you a visit.

Pretty much every person is overwhelmed, overworked, and simply over it during the month of December, when really, we should be overjoyed!

It's all in how we choose to look at things.

For example, instead of complaining about having to drive to three different locations on Christmas Day for separate celebrations, we should be thankful that we have so many wonderful family members who want to share Christmas with us. After all, many people find themselves all alone during the holidays. And instead of whining about having to work on Christmas Eve, we should be thankful that we have a job when so many folks are out of work this time of year. And rather than grumbling about the amount of Christmas parties and holiday happenings that we are obligated to attend, we should be grateful that we have friends and colleagues who value us enough to extend an invitation.

See how a small shift in thinking can make a big difference in our attitudes?

You know what else helps infuse joy into this season of stress? Being about the Father's business. When you're serving Him, it's energizing, not draining. It's not one more thing you HAVE to do; it's one more thing you GET to do. God will help you find time in even the craziest of schedules to ring a bell for the

Salvation Army or donate your time at a local soup kitchen or offer to babysit so that single mom you know can do her Christmas shopping.

Lastly, to feel more blessed and less stressed this month, start each day by praising God. And I mean, really get your praise on! Now this may seem extreme, but my sister shared this with me, and I want to share it with you. After my sister's husband died, she struggled to be happy in the morning. See, mornings were their time together—having their devotions and drinking coffee on the front porch.

With her husband gone, mornings felt empty...until she began worshipping the Lord. Though it felt a little silly at first, she started singing her favorite praise and worship songs and dancing before the Lord for the first ten minutes of the day. It completely transformed her life. She began looking forward to mornings again. She started each day with her heart full.

And so can you.

So if the Grinch has been sneaking around and trying to steal your contentment, joy, and peace this holiday season, send him right back up the chimney...and tell him to take his stress with him!

"Don't worry or stress. And always remember.

To focus on Jesus each day of December.

So, send the Grinch packing, and praise God each morn.

Rejoice because Jesus, our Savior, was born!"

Hearth to Heaven

"Lord God, help me to keep my eyes on You and to start each day giving You praise. And help me, Lord, to be a blessing to the people you put in my path today, and to realize that I am too blessed to be stressed. I love You. Amen."

A GIFT FROM GOD

"You will keep in perfect peace those whose minds are steadfast, because they trust in you."

ISAIAH 26:3, NIV

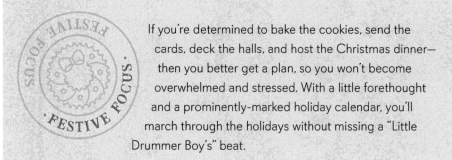

FESTIVE FOCUS

If you're determined to bake the cookies, send the cards, deck the halls, and host the Christmas dinner—then you better get a plan, so you won't become overwhelmed and stressed. With a little forethought and a prominently-marked holiday calendar, you'll march through the holidays without missing a "Little Drummer Boy's" beat.

Here are five tips to get you started:

 Use a wall chart that displays your Christmas parties, deadlines, appointments, etc. Cross off each one as you go and experience a sense of accomplishment!

 Give yourself a self-imposed deadline for sending out Christmas cards, buying gifts, shipping presents to out-of-town family, etc. Then try and hit each mark!

 Delegate for success! Call on your family members to help you get the job done. If your kids love wrapping presents, let them wrap the ones that aren't for them. If your husband is a good baker, put him on Christmas cookie duty.

 Allow for the unexpected! Remember, we live in the real world, which means things happen. So, don't wait until the last minute to tackle Christmas obligations. Allow for sickness, bad weather, unexpected visitors, etc.

 Give yourself a break! You'll need some downtime, so factor in a Spa Day during the holiday season. And don't forget to make time for Jesus. Don't cut your devotion time short in order to accomplish your "to do" list. After all, He is the reason for the season.

We Must Believe

By Andy Clapp

The Polar Express movie plays in our home multiple times each Christmas season. My girls love to watch it repeatedly. They sing along. They ask for hot chocolate while they sit on the couch. A few years ago, an opportunity to board a replica Polar Express opened up and my girls begged to take a ride.

We made our way to Spencer, North Carolina, and boarded the train, along with the other members of their Girl Scout troop. Their eyes lit up as they enjoyed the sounds of the night, they saw the beauty of the decorations, and with the faith of a child, they believed in the magic of the festivities.

The word "believe" played a prominent role in the events of the night. After we made our way home, the girls ran inside to play with the train that encircled our Christmas tree in the living room.

"Daddy, the train won't work," my oldest daughter explained, holding the engine with a look of disappointment.

"I really wanted to play with it," my youngest daughter added.

I took the engine from her hands and replaced the batteries. Two years prior, I had won the train in a white elephant game, probably my favorite gift I've ever won. I wanted one for my kids, for moments like these. Within seconds of a battery replacement, the sounds of joy, as well as the sounds of a locomotive, filled the air in our living room.

They smiled and sang while they played. I watched from a distance as their hearts overflowed with joy.

Just as the train is prominent in *The Polar Express*, trains have marked Christmas celebrations for years. In downtown Gibsonville, a small town neighboring where we live, a model train in the downtown area draws onlookers each year. The track is outlined in lights and winds down the rails and through the tunnels. The town also features an actual caboose outlined in white Christmas lights.

Hallmark movies often feature a train somewhere in the scenery. Who can forget the train in the hugely successful *White Christmas* with Bing Crosby and Danny Kaye? A train reunited George Bailey with his brother Harry in *It's A Wonderful Life*. Trains and Christmas naturally fit together in our holiday traditions. The engine of a train gives hope to reach the destination.

The engine that drives us is to believe this Christmas. Believe in the miracle of the season. Step out in faith and embrace the magnificent as the Lord brings us to another Christmas season. John wrote, *"But to all who did receive Him, He gave them the right to be children of God, to those who believe in His name"* (John 1:12, HCSB). It begins with believing that God loves us so much He sent His Son to come and die for us.

Believe in what God has done for you. Believe that the season offers more this year. The song of Bethlehem rings out to you today. All who believe in His name receive new life and a new identity as children of God. Mary put her faith in the words of an angel and the plan of God. Joseph trusted the message from

Each year, this classic film plays throughout the Christmas season. Fandango points out that in the film, *The Polar Express,* Tom Hanks plays seven different characters in the film. The next time you watch it, see if you can find all seven characters he played.[18]

FESTIVE FUN FACTS

God that came through the guidance of an angel in a dream. Throughout the history of humanity, faith moved mountains and changed lives.

What destination do you have in mind this Christmas? Are you longing for a deeper Christmas than years past? When the right engine drives your life, the right destination comes into view.

Throughout the season, we see trains. Whether it be in our towns, on our televisions, or around our Christmas tree, a train always comes into view. As we see them, let them be a reminder of the destination of Bethlehem. When you hear a train, let the sound of the wheels and engine remind us that what we believe should drive our celebration every Christmas.

Josh Groban's "Believe" assures the listener that if we believe, we have all that we need. In that truth, we board a train headed to the stable holding all we ever needed.

Our belief leads us to a place of worship and awe, as well as to fulfillment for what we already have in our lives.

Believe in Christ in such a way He stays central this Christmas and every day beyond. Faith leads us to the place of contentment in what we have.

Hearth to Heaven

"Heavenly Father, may we be moved by You this season. May what we believe drive all that we do at Christmas and throughout our lives. Thank You for giving us something amazing to believe in as we strive forward to our eternal destination with You."

A GIFT FROM GOD

"If you confess with your mouth, 'Jesus is Lord,' and believe in your heart
that God raised Him from the dead, you will be saved."

ROMANS 10:9, HCSB

Christmas Stories

By Michelle Medlock Adams

Every Christmas Eve when our daughters were young, we'd gather at my parents' house for fun and festivities. Then, right before it was time for the kids who still believed in Santa to go to bed, our daughters and their cousins would leave some of Mamaw's no-bake chocolate oatmeal cookies and a glass of milk on the kitchen counter for Santa. And that's not all. My dad, otherwise known as Papaw, would sit down with all of the grandkids and color a special picture for old Saint Nick. While coloring, I'd overhear Dad sharing about the night he almost caught Rudolph on the sundeck. Though my girls had heard that story many times, they never tired of it.

Neither did I.

You know what else I never grew tired of? When my father would grab his well-worn Bible and turn to the Gospel of Luke, Chapter 2, put on his reading glasses, and ask the family to gather in the living room. No one could read the Christmas Story quite like Dad. Whenever he got to verse 16 (NIV), *"So they hurried off and found Mary and Joseph, and the baby, who was lying in the manger,"* Dad would peer over his glasses and ask, "And that baby's name was?" And the kids would exclaim, "JESUS!"

In the craziness and commercialization of Christmas, it's more important than ever that we teach our children and share with our extended family the true reason for the season. Participating in fun family traditions involving Santa and his reindeer, and even the Elf on the Shelf, are fine…as long as we place our focus on the Manger.

Now that I have six grandbabies of my own, I can't wait to share Dad's Rudolph story, but even better, I can't wait to read the Christmas Story out of my well-worn Bible and ask that all-important question…

"And that baby's name was?"

Say it with me—JESUS!

Hearth to Heaven

"Father God, help me to keep the focus on You this Christmas, and help me to pass down my faith to my children and my grandchildren. Amen."

A GIFT FROM GOD

"I also did this so you could tell your children and your grandchildren about the miracles and other wonderful things that I have done in Egypt. Then all of you will know that I am the Lord."

EXODUS 10:2, ERV

Speaking of sharing stories...have you ever heard of the Twelve Books of Christmas tradition? If not, you've got to get in on it! Here's how it works. You choose twelve different Christmas children's books and read one book each night, leading up to Christmas Day. And to help you with your twelve book choices, I'm including some of my holiday favorites. (Full disclosure...I wrote a few of them!)

C is for Christmas by me, Michelle Medlock Adams, Illustrated by Louise Hargreaves. This picture book brings Jesus, Mary, Joseph, and the whole Nativity scene to life in a way that will teach littles about the best part of Christmas—Jesus!

M is for Manger by Crystal Bowman and Teri McKinley, Illustrated by Claire Keay. This rhyming storybook will soon be a family favorite that will entrance every reader in your home as it tells the story of Jesus chronologically.

Dachshund Through the Snow by me, Michelle Medlock Adams, and illustrated by Ana Sebastian encourages your teeny-tiniest kiddos to be confident in themselves as they cheer for Crosby in his quest to save Christmas.

That Grand Christmas Day by Jill Roman Lord, and illustrated by Alessia Trunfio builds up the Christmas story in rhyming verse to the big moment of Jesus' birth.

The Silent Noisy Night by Jill Roman Lord, Illustrated by Kelly Breemer. How could the night of the Savior's birth be silent if it was filled with animals and a baby? This book explores that thought through poetic verse.

A Birthday Party for Jesus by Susan Jones, Illustrated by Lee Holland. Learn about all the animals that celebrate Jesus every Christmas just by being together with Him. Kids will walk away from this book understanding that the true meaning of Christmas isn't presents or stockings, but the birth of Jesus.

5 More Sleeps 'til Christmas by Jimmy Fallon, Illustrated by Rich Deas. This fun book captures the anticipation of Christmas Day!

What is Christmas? by me, Michelle Medlock Adams, Illustrated by Amy Wummer. This board book is perfect for your youngest readers in the family. Fun art and engaging questions will help kids remember what Christmas is and what it isn't.

God Gave Us Christmas by Lisa Tawn Bergren, Illustrated by David Hohn. Follow a polar bear family learning the answers to questions the cubs have about Christmas. Children will walk away from this story knowing how much God loves them.

Christmas Love Letters from God by Glenys Nellist, Illustrated by Rachel Clowes. Explore passages from the Bible that reveal the story of Jesus in this book of both poetry and prose. Learn about God's promise for His children too!

Humphrey's First Christmas written and illustrated by Carol Heyer. Follow Humphrey the camel on his long, cold journey to Bethlehem to meet Jesus. Children will learn the importance of Christmas and better understand gift giving.

Jesus Calling: The Story of Christmas by Sarah Young, Illustrated by Katya Longhi. This picture book shows children that God always had a plan for Christmas.

The Bells Ring Out This Time of Year

By Andy Clapp

The sound of bells at Christmas strikes up a harmony in our hearts, the song of souls thankful for the Savior that came.

Bell-shaped cookies sit on platters at parties. Handbell services echo from church buildings. Church bells ring out the sounds of the season for all to hear. Sleigh bells jingle and volunteers ring bells on behalf of the Salvation Army.

Bells chime at the end of *It's a Wonderful Life* when an angel receives his wings. At our home, bells hang on our tree to remind us of those loved ones who are no longer with us on earth but who are part of each Christmas we share.

We even sing about bells at Christmas time. The beloved carol "Silver Bells" plays throughout the season. My favorite classic is a hymn titled "I Heard the Bells on Christmas Day." Most know the song, but few know the story behind it. Once I learned the history, the song took on even more meaning in my life.

The words came from the famous American poet, Henry Wadsworth Longfellow. The date of the song ties back to the Civil War period. Longfellow's sorrow marks some of the lyrics of the song. He had experienced the death of his first wife and his second wife. His son had enlisted in the Civil War, leaving the poet on edge

"Jingle Bells" serves as one of the most recognizable tunes of the season. Its chorus happens to be one of the first Christmas songs learned by children. But, according to History.com, the song's original title was "One Horse Open Sleigh."[20]

and dreading the possibility of his son perishing on the battlefield.

He wrote of no peace being present in the situation. His wartime poem expressed the ugliness of his current reality steeped in prevailing hate. Near the end, however, he heard the bells again. In that instance, the ringing reminded him of the presence, faithfulness, and righteousness of God.[19]

Amazing how Christmas reminds us of God's faithfulness in a way no other season can. Just to hear the bells of the Salvation Army or the bells of a church reminds us that a special time is here.

The sound of Christmas rings and solidifies the truths that God is able and that He is near and that His presence fills the air. The sound of the first Christmas began with a song of Mary's heart, a praise of what God had done. She praised, *My soul proclaims the greatness of the Lord, and my spirit has rejoiced in God my Savior* (Luke 1:46-47, HCSB). Angelic sounds filled the air on the night Jesus was born. Praise emanated from hearts amazed at the miracle of Bethlehem.

A song of hope arose.

Bells are the sound of Christmas each year, calling us to a place of peace, a time of joy, a season of love. From the chime of each bell, we embrace the announcement that an arrival comes! The heavens fill with the sound of their ringing, their song leading to a new song in our hearts each December.

With each ringing, with each pealing of the bells, a reminder comes. God calls out each Christmas to remind us that He is near and there is life to be embraced. Hope rings loud and clear reminding us that this season centers around Christ's coming to the earth. Just as Longfellow found inspiration from the bells, their tune proclaiming a loving God, we find such an inspiration ourselves.

Do you hear the beauty of the Christmas bells? Ring a bell this season, a proclamation that death and despair give way to life and joy today.

Hearth to Heaven

"Heavenly Father, open our ears to hear the bells of Christmas, the melody of triumph our souls desire today! May we ring with joy the story of Jesus and carry that song with us to a broken world. In Jesus' name we pray, Amen."

A GIFT FROM GOD

"And Mary said: My soul proclaims the greatness of the Lord, and my spirit has rejoiced in God my Savior, because He has looked with favor on the humble condition of His slave. Surely, from now on all generations will call me blessed, because the Mighty One has done great things for me, and His name is holy."

LUKE 1:46-49, HCSB

A Crafty Christmas

By Michelle Medlock Adams

As our family grew, my sister and I decided it might be easier on everyone's bank accounts if we started drawing names for Christmas. That way, we wouldn't have to buy presents for every person in our extended family, only the person's name that we chose out of the hat. We tried that for one year, but many of us ended up buying every person a present anyway, which defeated the whole purpose of the name drawing. Then, my sister had, what she thought, was a brilliant idea.

"Let's have a crafty Christmas!" she declared that Thanksgiving. "Let's all agree to use our talents and make gifts this year."

And so, the crafty Christmas planning began. My niece Autumn decided to make candles. My other niece Mandy put her creativity to work making picture frames. My daughter Allyson decided to make original jewelry pieces for each family member. My daughter Abby planned to use her calligraphy skills to create personalized wall hangings. Jeff and I decided we would make fleece tie-blankets. And my sister Martie planned to mix up a batch of her secret beauty lotion, otherwise known as "Pink Fluff," and then decorate adorable containers of her magic concoction for each of us.

Jeff and I finished the final tie-blanket just in time for our first ever Crafty Christmas. Some of the sides weren't exactly even, but it was the best we could do.

As it turned out, everyone's creations were a bit "off." All of the gifts were made with a lot of heart…just not a lot of talent. I think my sister overestimated our abilities when she came up with the Crafty Christmas idea. In fact, our daughters still refer to that year as the "Crappy Christmas," lol. But I think back on that Christmas and smile, and I still treasure those gifts. We learned that our handmade gifts didn't have to be perfect to make the recipient feel perfectly loved.

Every time I burned the candle that Autumn made or wore the cuff bracelet that Ally created, I felt truly loved. See, I knew that every crafty Christmas gift had taken a substantial amount of time to make, and just knowing that fact, made each present even more meaningful.

That must be how God feels when we take time to offer Him our gifts, not just at Christmas but every day of the year. For example, even if you don't have the loveliest singing-voice, when you offer up praises to Him, God loves it! He doesn't even care if you sing offkey. And when you get up a little earlier in the morning just to spend time with Him (even if you doze off once or twice during your Bible reading), He still loves it. God knows we're imperfect. He knows we won't always get it right. But He loves us just the same. He loves your praises, your efforts, and your giftings. So make sure that in all of your gifting this year, that you don't neglect your Heavenly Father.

Hearth to Heaven

"Heavenly Father, help me to make time to praise You and simply be in Your presence, and Lord, please use my giftings for Your Kingdom. I give You my whole heart. I love You. Amen."

A Gift from God

"And remember the words of the Lord Jesus, that He said,
'It is more blessed to give than to receive'."

ACTS 20:35, NKJV

FESTIVE FOCUS

If you're short on cash but long on creativity—you can give wonderful homemade gifts from the heart this Christmas. Not the kind of homemade gifts that cause the recipient to say, "Thanks, you shouldn't have. Really you shouldn't have."

No, you can make Christmas gifts that will be priceless to those receiving them. Think about it, your parents still display the lopsided pot you sculpted in third grade! Why? Because they love you and treasure everything that you've ever created for them.

So with that in mind, use whatever artistic abilities you have and make something special for the special people on your gift list. If you're a writer, craft a poem expressing your appreciation and love in each line. Remember, poetry doesn't have to rhyme so don't stress out if you're not very good at the rhyme game. Just write from your heart. Then, package your poem in a beautiful frame or place it on the inside cover of a photo album or a decorative journal.

If you're an artist, why not paint a picture of a favorite family memory? Then, frame it so that your loved one can display it in a place of prominence. Or do several drawings that illustrate your loved one's favorite scriptures and write the corresponding verse beneath each drawing. Title it, "God's Promises for You!" Now, that's a gift!

Don't panic if you're not a poet or a painter. If you can cut and paste, you have all of the needed skills to make a truly great scrapbook for your sentimental mama. Gather photographs from long ago (you may need other family members' assistance acquiring photos), as well as current pictures, and organize them chronologically or by occasion. Then, write humorous and sweet captions for each photo. You might even want to buy sticker packs that are specifically made for photo albums (the kind that won't fade or bleed onto your pictures) to add pizzazz to your pages.

If you're creating a sentimental scrapbook for your spouse, you might paste past concert tickets, pressed flowers from an anniversary gone by, programs from shared plays and events, and other special mementos. He will love it. He may not admit it, but he'll love it!

Yes, those homemade gifts all take time—some more than others—so, if you haven't any money to buy a great gift nor the time to make one, don't despair. If you have fifteen minutes, you can create "Love Coupons!" Love Coupons can be anything from, "I promise to mow your yard for an entire month" to "This coupon is good for two dozen of my world-famous chocolate chip cookies." You know your loved ones better than anyone, so make the coupons redeemable for their favorite things. For a nice presentation, write the coupons on construction paper and secure them with a pretty holiday ribbon. For more DIY Christmas gift ideas, check out the "80 DIY Holiday Presents Your Friends and Family Won't Decide to Re-Gift" in the footnotes.[21]

Do You See What I See?

By Andy Clapp

Even the darkest winter's night cannot douse the lights of the Christmas season.

Each year, we set out for a drive to McAdenville, North Carolina. Lights hang and glow in our town but a trip to the place nicknamed "Christmas Town, USA" is essential.

The entire town stands aglow. Visitors from neighboring cities, as well as folks from other states, take a drive through the majestic city that comes alive each December. As new arrivals descend the hill into the town, lights surround them, adding to the festiveness of the season.

The tradition began in 1956. Volunteers carried out the work of transforming the southern Piedmont town into the Christmas Town people flock to see. McAdenville opens its arms for all to come as there is no admission fee to see the breathtaking lights. So many light festivals charge per car that enters, yet McAdenville remains free. The residents welcome onlookers. The town bids for all to come.

So they do. According to WBTV, about 500,000 people drive through the village each Christmas season.[22] The view at the lake draws every eye to catch a glimpse, to absorb a few seconds and carry it throughout the year. Around the lake trees stand aglow with illuminated decorations, thousands of lights piercing a winter's night. Yet, the reflection captivates so many.

Upon the waters, the lights reflect. The vibrant scene emerges on the surface of the lake, forcing all to stop and take it in. Of all the beauty of the town, the lake and its reflection serve as a highlight. Passersby take pictures, trying to capture a moment when they were captivated and in awe.

Christmas is a celebration that the light of the world came for us in Bethlehem. Not only did He come, but in His coming, a world mired in darkness received an invitation to come and see. Chris Tomlin and Lauren Daigle's "Noel" speaks to this very aspect. We are implored to come and see what God did when He sent the Light.

So much Scripture deals with light. In the opening of the gospel of John, the disciple wrote, *"The true light, who gives light to everyone, was coming into the world"* (John 1:9,

HCSB). The light came and offered light and life to all. To each, an invitation was extended to come and see. Later in His ministry, Jesus said, *"I am the light of the world. Anyone who follows Me will never walk in the darkness but will have the light of life"* (John 8:12, HCSB).

The light of the world beckons every soul to come and see. From the beginning, a night sky pierced with angelic light called to the outcasts. The light of a star led those with watchful eyes to the place where they would find the Savior of the world. Later, the Light of the World called anyone who longed to escape the darkness to follow Him and find the light of life.

Light reveals that which cannot be found in the darkness. Light signifies fellowship with sight. The Light of the World calls each of us to come

According to Attractions of America, the biggest display of lights in North America is found at Busch Gardens in Williamsburg, Virginia. Busch Gardens is laid out with a European theme, featuring sections of the park dedicated to Germany, England, Scotland, and more. In December, the theme park transforms into a brilliant light display, boasting more than eight million Christmas lights.[23]

and see what God has done and to walk in the light rather than the darkness. The lights of a small town attract visitors from great distances. The invitation comes without a cost. As the Light of the World came, He offered the free gift of eternal life.

As the light shines again this season, see the way it brings life to the streets of each town or city through which you travel. When the lights of the season surround you, when you are immersed in the splendor of their glow, think of the Light of the World. Take each light display as an invitation to come and see what happened in Bethlehem.

Lighting the way to new life, shining in the darkness to reveal the snares against you, Jesus calls you to walk in the light and to be the light of the world. When you shine for Him, you reflect His light. It's then that you extend the invitation for others to see what the Lord has done in your life.

Hearth to Heaven

"Heavenly Father, thank You for the light You provide in this darkened world. Thank you for sending the Light of this world, Jesus Christ, to Bethlehem. Help us to shine for You each day and extend the invitation for others to come and see what You have done. In Jesus' name we pray, Amen."

A GIFT FROM GOD

"Then Jesus spoke to them again: "I am the light of the world. Anyone who follows Me will never walk in the darkness but will have the light of life"

JOHN 8:12, HCSB

The Angel Tree

By Michelle Medlock Adams

We were running late for church…again.

"Oh, good. They're still singing," I whispered to my husband as we hurried through the foyer, each with a daughter in hand.

"Look at the pretty Christmas trees!" squealed Ally, our then-four-year-old.

"Yes, I love all of the white lights," I answered, still hurrying.

"What are those?" asked Ally, pointing to the little tags hanging on each of the branches.

"They're angels!" Abby, our then-five-year-old, answered her little sister.

"Yeah, but what's all that writing on the angels' heads?" Ally continued.

"Oh, well that is the name of each of the angels in heaven," Abby answered, matter-of-factly.

My husband and I smiled at each other upon hearing Abby's very sure, very wrong answer, but neither of us had the heart to correct her at that moment. Plus, we were too late for a discussion, so we smiled at our girls, and quickly grabbed seats in the back of the sanctuary. Later in the service, our pastor explained the meaning of the Angel Tree and urged each of us to take angel tags and purchase gifts for those children who wouldn't receive Christmas presents any other way. After the closing hymn, the girls rushed out to the Angel Tree and grabbed one angel tag each.

The next few weeks were filled with lots of holiday fanfare—Christmas plays, Christmas cards, Christmas cookies, Christmas parties, and so much more. But in the midst of the hustle and bustle of the season, we also went shopping for our "angels."

Each angel card listed the child's sizes, favorite toys, and most-desired present. After we filled the cart with every item on the angels' respective lists, I high-fived the girls for a job well done. I was amazed at how excited my girls were to be shopping for others! After all, they had made out their Christmas wish lists way back in October, circling practically every item on each catalogue page. But on that day, running through the

If your church doesn't put up an Angel Tree during the holidays, you might ask if you could organize such a tree. Or you could stop by your local Salvation Army and see if your local chapter participates in the National Salvation Army Angel Tree program. Through this option, children and senior adults who qualify are registered and accepted into the program, and you can adopt them and shop for them—just like we did through our church.

And doesn't every person—especially children—deserve to experience pure joy on Christmas morning? And here's the win/win—you and your family will also experience pure joy by purchasing and wrapping those special gifts for your assigned angels. To learn more, go to https://saangeltree.org/online.[24]

store's aisles, shopping for their angels, my girls weren't at all concerned about their presents. In fact, as we approached the checkout line, Ally begged me to buy fuzzy slippers for her angel too, even though they weren't on the list.

For years, we had read the Christmas story to our daughters, explaining how God had given His very best gift when He sent Jesus. They'd nod as if they understood, but I was afraid they were getting caught up in the commercialism of Christmas and forgetting the true meaning of the Christmas story. I feared they wouldn't understand the sacrifice God had made for us. I worried they would grow up being takers, not givers simply because we'd given them so much. But at that moment, when Ally begged me to buy fuzzy slippers, I realized my girls were grasping the joy of giving and honoring the true spirit of Christmas. And that was the best gift I could've ever received.

As we wrapped every present for the angels we'd adopted, we sang a few Christmas carols and munched on more than a few Christmas cookies. Abby made special curly bows for the top of each package, and Ally insisted we add glitter. We delivered the gifts for our angels the following Sunday, placing them under the big Christmas tree in the church foyer. The girls' giggles filled the air as tears filled my eyes. I thought it might be nice to pray over the gifts before we left, so I asked Abby and Ally to do so. Abby passed, and Ally kept it short and sweet:

"Dear God, help this be the bestest Christmas ever for our angels. Amen."

I don't know if it ended up being the "bestest" Christmas ever for our angels, but it certainly was for us. It was the year we learned it truly is better to give than to receive, and it was the year that set the tone for all of our future Christmases.

May this Christmas be your bestest ever!

Hearth to Heaven

"Father God, help me to give more than I take in this world. And help me to notice those who are less fortunate than I am and see them through Your eyes. Use me today, Lord, to bless others. I love You. Amen."

A GIFT FROM GOD

"Whoever despises his neighbor is a sinner, but blessed is he who is generous to the poor."

PROVERBS 14:21, ESV

Day 23

A Candy with a Purpose

By Andy Clapp

What would Christmas be without candy?

The most iconic and recognizable candy of the season is the candy cane. Of all the different options for Christmas candies, the candy cane shouts that Christmas is near. Some hang the candy cane on their tree. Almost every mall Santa gives them out to children who stop by for a visit. Candy canes adorn the outside of gifts. Just as these candies make Christmas special, they also point to what makes Christmas significant.

Legend holds that a candy maker created the candy cane with the gospel in mind. A shepherd's crook-shape reminds us of the Great Shepherd.[25] The white represents the purity of Christ while the red stripes remind us of the blood Jesus shed. When understood, the candy cane becomes a story, telling of the greatest story from its color and shape.

A few years ago, we searched for a way to help children share their faith with others. Having six-year-olds memorize the Romans Road seemed daunting so we turned to the candy cane. We developed Christmas boxes with devotions and activities, including tools for learning the symbols of the candy cane. Each child received two candy canes. One was for them to enjoy. The second was for the children to give to someone else and tell the story.

In mere days, a tiny army of ambassadors for Christ spread the story to others.

107

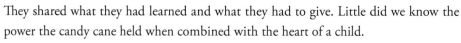

They shared what they had learned and what they had to give. Little did we know the power the candy cane held when combined with the heart of a child.

"Can I give Grammy my candy cane," my youngest daughter asked.

"Sure," I replied, "but you also have to tell her what it means."

She began to explain to her grandmother the symbols of the candy cane. A few hiccups didn't stop her. When stumped, she turned to me and my wife for a reminder.

At the end, she beamed as she handed off the candy cane. I rejoiced as I listened to my daughter share Jesus.

Sharing the story of Christmas brings us to a place of worship. So amazed are we at what God has done that we want others to hear. We glorify the Lord by telling others of who He is, how He loves, and how His faithfulness surpasses anything else we experience on earth.

An angel's words, followed by a sky filled with a multitude of the heavenly hosts, demanded their audience tell what they saw. The shepherds shared the details with Mary and Joseph. How could you hold in such an experience? Judging by the shepherd's actions, they had to tell somebody.

Can you imagine the excitement they showed sharing the story? Luke wrote, *"After seeing them, they reported the message they were told about this child, and all who heard it were amazed at what the shepherds said to them"* (Luke 2:17-18, HCSB). Those who experienced one of many remarkable moments passed the joy on to others. I imagine each one was excited that not only could they share the story, but that people listened to them for once.

Given the chance, witnesses to these majesties shared every word they heard. The angel said this Child was the Savior of the world. The angel pointed them to the exact

Child they needed to find. Shepherds, notoriously overlooked, rejoiced in the moment they received an invitation. Luke tells us that they passed on what the angels told them about Jesus. And I assure you, they passed it on to anyone who listened during the rest of their lives.

An unlikely visit opened the door for the shepherds to share a story. For our children, a simple piece of candy helped them to become the missionaries we are all called to be. What will you use to tell the story, not only this Christmas but every day from here onward? To share of what the Lord has done should be as normal to a Christian as breathing.

Christ came. His first set of visitors were outcasts. They shared their experience because from just the invitation alone, they knew God cared for them.

He cares about us as well. The fact that He offers eternal life calls us to Him, gives us a story to tell the world.

As Christmas comes and goes, our testimony remains valuable in all seasons. Take a candy cane, share it with others, and explain to them how Jesus can change their lives. Who knew candy could open the door to eternity?

It's time for us to share with the world!

We hang them from trees, attach them to presents, receive them from Santa, and find them in our stockings. There are entire aisles in the store with nothing but different styles, sizes, and flavors of candy canes. According to Where Y'at, there are nearly two billion candy canes produced each year. Just as interesting is the fact that National Candy Cane Day isn't until December 26th.[26]

Hearth to Heaven

"Heavenly Father, give us the heart of those shepherds this Christmas and beyond. As You have given us so much, stoke a fire within us to share Your story with others. Open the door for us to give the world the sweetest gift this Christmas—the gift of knowing Jesus Christ. In Jesus' name we pray, Amen."

A GIFT FROM GOD

"But He was wounded for our transgressions, He was bruised for our iniquities;
The chastisement for our peace was upon Him, and by His stripes we are healed."

ISAIAH 53:5, NKJV

The Ugly Christmas Sweater

By Michelle Medlock Adams

I'll never forget that morning. I was loading the dishwasher when my youngest daughter, Ally, called downstairs: "Hey Mom, can I borrow your redbird sweater?" I was sure I must've misheard her. After all, my fashionista daughter rarely thought anything I wore was fashion-forward.

"My new Christmas sweater?" I asked, making my way upstairs to find it for her.

"That's the one," she answered, already searching through my closet.

"Here it is," I said, reaching over her shoulder. "Oh, and I bought sparkly cardinal earrings to go with it. You're welcome to borrow those too."

"Just the sweater is fine." Ally smiled and headed out of my room.

The morning was busy with client calls, but I spent the afternoon decorating our front porch with greenery, Christmas pillows, white lights, and more. After all, it was the first week of December, and I was definitely getting into the holiday spirit. I was even sporting one of my holiday sweatshirts that featured the Grinch and the saying, "Merry Grinchmas."

Just then, Jeff poked his head out the front door. "Hey, are you ready? We need to leave for the game."

I glanced down at my phone and couldn't believe it was 6:30 already. Both of our daughters were cheerleaders for the Bedford North Lawrence High School Stars, and

Ever wonder where the Ugly Christmas Sweater tradition began? There are several theories, but the one that seems to be the most prominent, dates back to 2002. Two men from Vancouver came up with the idea to host the first official tacky holiday sweater party as a fundraiser for their friend's cancer treatment. It was a huge hit! And that's where it all began.

Today, Ugly Christmas Sweater parties take place in workplaces, churches, schools, and charity events all over the world. There are even competitions for the very ugliest sweater in communities nationwide, and people go all out! Some sweaters are wired to light up. Some glow in the dark. Some are edible. Still, others are musical! And all of them are...ugly.[27]

Jeff and I never missed a game.

"I'll just have to go as is," I mumbled, pointing to my Grinch sweatshirt. "I'm not very school spirit-y."

"True, but you're very holiday spirit-y," Jeff teased as we headed to the high school.

As we made our way through the gym, I could not believe my eyes! It seemed everyone had the Christmas spirit that night. So many Christmas sweaters...mostly on students.

"Hey, Kenzie," I greeted one of the girls from church. "Look how cute you are! Love your fuzzy candy cane sweater!"

"Right?" she said. "Watch this!"

Then she pushed something on her sweater, and it started blinking! It was a light-up Christmas sweater! I was so impressed, and a bit envious.

"I love it!" I marveled.

"Isn't it the best?" she beamed. "I can't believe I didn't win."

"Win...win what?" I asked.

"Oh," she said, "It was Ugliest Christmas Sweater Day at school today. I think Ally might've placed with her bird sweater…well, see ya!"

It didn't take Jeff long to figure out what had transpired, and he laughed so hard, that I didn't think he would make it up the bleachers to our seats.

Needless to say, the Christmas redbird sweater went to Goodwill the following week, but I kept my Merry Grinchmas sweatshirt, and I still wear it every holiday season with pride. And I have added a few other "ugly Christmas sweaters" to my collection over the years. I have one with the cutest wiener dog on it that says, "Dachshund Through the Snow," which is really special, since it's the title of my latest children's holiday picture book. And I even had a podcast host who discovered my obsession with festive fashion—particularly Christmas sweaters—make a one-of-a-kind light-up Christmas sweater for me, featuring gaudy tinsel and plush holiday-themed animals. I love it! I'm pretty sure nobody is going to ask to borrow that one! But you can bet I'll be wearing it on the third Friday of December this year— that's when our country celebrates National Ugly Christmas Sweater Day.

You know, ugly Christmas sweaters are a great reminder of why we have Christmas—because we needed a Savior to leave the perfection of heaven, come to earth as a baby, grow up, and die on a cross for our ugly sin (John 3:16). Jesus, the

Light of the world, exposed the ugliness of man's sin, and then He offered His beautiful, unconditional love to us so that we could spend eternity in heaven with Him.

If you haven't ever given your heart to Jesus and made Him the Lord of your life, today is your day! All you have to do is pray this prayer with me: "Father God, thank You for sending Jesus to die on a cross for my ugly sins. I admit that I'm a sinner, and I repent. Please come into my heart, Lord. I make You my Lord and Savior. I love You, and I want to serve You the rest of my life. Help me, Lord, to be a light in this dark world. Amen."

Now go out there and let your light shine for Jesus. Don't hide it under a bushel… or an ugly Christmas sweater.

Hearth to Heaven

"Father God, help me to let my light shine for You, and help me to be able to witness to those who so desperately need You. Amen."

A Gift from God

"In the same way, let your light shine before others, that they may see your good deeds and glorify your Father in heaven."

MATTHEW 5:16, NIV

A Plant of Christmas Colors

By Andy Clapp

Red and green, the colors of the season, come alive in the wrapped pots holding poinsettias.

Each year, dozens of these festive flowers cover the front of the church, lining the piano and the organ. The red petals and green leaves point to the season in a way most plants cannot. Each poinsettia at our church is given in honor or memory of someone.

The list is included in each week's bulletin, a four-week reminder of the person's importance. The beauty of the plant comes with a beautiful memory or dedication attached.

One year, my dedication read "In Memory of Manlis Gordon from Andy Clapp." After my grandfather's passing, I wanted something to be a reminder of him in the church. He valiantly fought in World War II, so he stood larger than life in my eyes. During the season, the poinsettia with his name reminded me of him each service.

"In honor of my mother" another note reads as one of the congregants places a poinsettia at the front.

The rise of the poinsettia in American culture began with a United States ambassador to Mexico. Joel Poinsett saw the plant in Mexico then brought the plants home to his greenhouses in South Carolina. As he gave them away, their popularity grew. Now, poinsettias are seen throughout the United States, especially around Christmas.

Their connection with Christmas comes from an old Mexican legend. A young girl, Pepita, bound by poverty, had no gift to give to baby Jesus. As the Christmas Eve service approached, her despair grew and on the way to the service, her cousin Pedro encouraged her to give Jesus anything she could find as a gift.

The poor Mexican girl plucked a handful of weeds and made an arrangement. She laid the flowers at the altar, and as legend holds, her gift of weeds exploded into a bouquet with red flowers. The legend says that those in attendance believed it to be a miracle.[28]

The poinsettia features symbols that speak to the true meaning of Christmas. The shape of the leaves is similar to what is believed to be the shape of the star of Bethlehem. The red of the leaves spoke to the blood of Jesus Christ while the white signifies the purity of Christ. The very nature of the flower causes us to stop and remember Jesus.

For the Wise Men, a star stopped them and then moved them. The angels halted the shepherds and invited them into the event's majesty. Mary experienced a visit from an angel while Joseph experienced an angel in his dream. After the day passed, each one had something to stop and remind them of Jesus. But most prominent was Mary's remembrance. Luke records, *"But Mary was treasuring up all these things in her heart and meditating on them"* (Luke 2:19, HCSB).

Those stories replayed in her mind. They reminded her of the miracle God performed when Jesus came to the earth. She held tight to each detail for it was part of something never to be forgotten. I believe she never passed a stable again without thinking about that night in Bethlehem. A miracle, *the* miracle, shines hope throughout life, and therefore cannot be forgotten or overlooked.

To all of us, God's work stands as nothing short of miraculous and must be remembered. We easily remember when life doesn't go our way but too easily forget the miraculous works of the Lord in our lives when life is smooth sailing. The same can be said of Christmas. We focus on the festivities more than the faith. We emphasize making memories but neglect to remember the miraculous happenings of Bethlehem.

We are accustomed to poinsettias being the size of a small house plant. Many are contained in plastic containers, wrapped in green or red foil at the base of the plant to enhance the festiveness of the poinsettia. However, the poinsettia, in its native environment in Central America and Mexico, can grow much taller than the poinsettias we are accustomed to seeing. In the tropical environment, they can grow to 10-15 feet in height.[29]

The poinsettia is a plant that features many symbols of Christmas and is, according to legend, a miracle in and of itself. As we look at the beautiful plant, we remember the beauty of Bethlehem, the truth of the Savior, the moment of the miracle. While so much draws our attention away from the meaning, God gave us the best there was as His Son came to walk with us.

Let's fill our hearts and lives with what reminds us of the miracles that unfolded.

The birth of Christ is what fulfills the soul in this season and beyond. The poinsettia reminds us of a legendary miracle, pointing us back to the truly miraculous time of a Savior born in Bethlehem.

Hearth to Heaven

"Heavenly Father, fill our hearts, minds, and eyes with that which reminds us of the truly miraculous. Let it be about the birth of Christ and keep in our minds the miracle work You've done in our lives. Your work truly amazes us. Let us not be distracted away from the greatness of what You've done."

A GIFT FROM GOD

"But Mary was treasuring up all these things in her heart and meditating on them."
LUKE 2:19, HCSB

Mistletoe All Year Round

By Michelle Medlock Adams

Mistletoe is a beautiful plant. Its distinctive green leaves and white berries are so striking. It's easy to see why people love hanging it over their doorways as part of their Christmas décor—and thinking of it as a symbol of peace and love!

Something you might not know about mistletoe, though, is that it doesn't die at the end of winter. Mistletoe is an evergreen, so those bright green leaves stay just as beautiful long after the Christmas decorations are put away.

We don't usually think about mistletoe throughout the rest of the year, though, do we? We may hang sprigs of it in our homes for the holidays, but when thinking of beautiful plants for spring, summer, and fall, mistletoe never comes to mind.

In fact, we might completely forget about mistletoe once the snow melts, but nature certainly doesn't. Many organisms depend on it to survive. Some species of mistletoe are considered "keystone species," which are species that are so integral to their ecosystems that removing them would be catastrophic to their environments. Deer, squirrels, and porcupines rely on its berries for food. Birds use its branches to make nests. Butterflies use the leaves as a place to lay their eggs. Bees need it to harvest nectar. In the UK, mistletoe is a protected plant under the Wildlife and Countryside Act because removing too much of it could completely throw off the balance of the ecosystems in which it resides. Isn't it crazy that we can so easily forget about such an important plant simply because the holidays are over?

That started me thinking…what other parts of Christmas do we forget about once the calendar changes to a New Year? If we're being honest, I think sometimes we do the same thing with Jesus. During December, we think about the Christmas story all the time. The month is filled with images of shepherds and angels and mangers. But when the nativity scene is packed away, we stop re-reading and studying the Christmas story, as if it's only for seasonal occasions.

But like mistletoe, the Christmas story is such an important piece of the bigger picture, giving so much meaning to the rest of Scripture. Without the Christmas story, we wouldn't know about Mary's heart, or John the Baptist's heritage, or the prophesies that were fulfilled when Jesus was born. Without the Christmas story, we wouldn't have the birth of Christ, His death and resurrection, or the gift of salvation and eternal life. Without the Christmas story, we would still be lost in a broken world, with no joy, no peace, and no hope.

You see, the nativity isn't just a Christmas decoration; it's the introduction to the greatest story ever told, and the cornerstone of our faith.

> FESTIVE FUN FACTS · FESTIVE FUN FACTS
>
> There are 1,500 species of mistletoe. European mistletoe (the kind we usually see at Christmastime) is scientifically known as *Viscum album*. These are its genus and species according to taxonomic rank. But can you guess its order category? It's in the order Santalales. Yes, like Santa Claus! Maybe it's so popular at Christmastime because Saint Nicholas liked its name so much! [30]

There's one more important attribute to keep in mind about mistletoe: it thrives in light. A lot of times you can find it growing on the open branches of apple trees, hawthorn trees, and poplar trees. But you won't find it growing in a forest, where the sunlight is blocked. It can't survive in dark places. If you were to keep a sprig of mistletoe packed away in storage boxes, only to be brought out as a Christmas decoration, it would die. Mistletoe thrives in light—much like we thrive in the presence of the Light of the World.

So don't pack away your faith until next Christmas. Keep the Christmas story alive and well in your heart, today, and all year through.

Hearth to Heaven

"Father God, I thank You for sending Your Son down to earth to live among us. What an incredible act of love. Help me to never forget Your precious gift of Jesus. Amen."

A GIFT FROM GOD

"Be careful that you do not forget the Lord your God, failing to observe his commands, his laws and his decrees that I am giving you this day."

DEUTERONOMY 8:11, NIV

The Man Behind the Legend

By Andy Clapp

A caricature overtook the truth, a legendary tale overshadowing what is known about a sacrificial person.

Saint Nicholas is more than a mere fairy tale. A bishop whose roots trace to Greece, not the North Pole, Saint Nick made an impact on lives in the late third and early fourth centuries. His story began with tragedy, but his heart and conviction turned the story to triumph. Nicholas lost his parents at an early age, but before their death, they instilled in him a foundation of faith.

His faith foundation paved the way for the rest of his life. Inside Nicholas beat a heart of sacrifice. Rather than wallow in his loss, he looked outward to see the pain of those around him. He saw an opportunity to serve, a chance to make a lasting impact. Nicholas took a blessing, his inheritance, and provided for those who were in need. He saw what he possessed as something that could bless others.

Nicholas faced persecution later. As Christians became targets, he endured imprisonment but emerged after, still motivated by his faith. As time continued, even after his death, people shared the story of this generous man who gave of what he had to help the people around him. His life knew tragedy and struggle. His legacy, however, is one of ultimate victory.

Learning the truth about Saint Nicholas inspires us this Christmas. Given reasons to wallow in what had transpired, he chose to rise up and make a difference. His heart of love and charity left a legacy, a story that continues to be shared sixteen-hundred years after his passing. He used what he had. Others benefited greatly.

His life presents a depiction of the story and the Spirit of Christmas which carries beyond a single day.

Christmas, more than any other time of the year, leads us to bless other people. Be it first responders, teachers, faith leaders, friends, or our hairstylist, we give without hesitation as Christmas draws near.

St. Nicholas church in Myra was built on the foundations of an older church where Nicholas served as a bishop. The original church structure was affected by the shifting of the river pattern in the area.[31]

Does it really take the decorations to open our eyes to see how blessed we are? Does the calendar dictate when we can be blessings?

Throughout Scripture, God blessed His people, whether they deserved it or not. Even while in rebellion, God blessed humanity. He provided manna. He split the Red Sea. The Creator provided for the needs of the creation. But in Bethlehem, God took giving to a whole new level.

John wrote, *"He was in the world, and the world was created through Him, yet the world did not recognize Him. He came to His own people, and His own people did not receive Him"* (John 1:10-11, HCSB). God sent His son into the world. Jesus gave up heaven to walk the earth and die for the sins of humanity. John explained later that we received grace after grace through Jesus.

Life guarantees we will experience struggles, afflictions, trials, and pains. How do we react? Jesus blessed others though He would go to the cross and die. He gave grace, forgiveness, and salvation, even to those who killed Him. Saint Nicholas endured pain from the loss of his parents and suffered persecution because of his faith. Yet, he blessed others with the blessings he received.

We overcome evil with good. We triumph over tragedy by blessing others in need of a blessing. What we gained from Bethlehem cannot be measured. What we have is most often more than we need on this earth, so we have the opportunity to tell a bigger and better story.

The heart that understands Christmas is a heart that longs to bless others. We see how no matter our situation, we are blessed with a Savior. We can be a Nicholas to those in our lives by giving to others from that which Jesus blesses us with each day. We can look beyond what we experience to improve what others are going through in their lives.

How can what you have change the life of someone around you? Take that question with you throughout the year and watch the Lord open doors for you to help others.

Hearth to Heaven

"Heavenly Father, You have blessed us beyond measure. You have given us so much. Show us how to use what You have blessed us with to be a blessing for others. Give us a heart to bless others and point them to You in the process. In Jesus' name we pray, Amen."

A GIFT FROM GOD

"He was in the world, and the world was created through Him, yet the world did not recognize Him. He came to His own, and His own people did not receive Him."

JOHN 1:10-11, HCSB

The Art of Christmas Caroling

By Michelle Medlock Adams

Is there anything that puts you in the Christmas mood quite like the sound of Christmas carols? Maybe you're the kind of person who loves going caroling door-to-door, singing your way through your neighborhood, and personally sharing Christmas cheer. Maybe you prefer to quietly sit near a fire, listening to the carolers with a cup of cocoa in your hand. Or maybe you're like me and enjoy a little bit of both!

No matter how you choose to partake in Christmas caroling this year, I think there's a lot we can learn from those melodic messengers. Sure, the songs are pretty, but the act of caroling can symbolize so much more about the season.

First, it's impossible to carol quietly.

Sharing the good news of Christ should not be a quiet calling. It's not something you murmur or whisper. It's the kind of news you want to shout from the rooftops, right? Can you imagine carolers coming to your door and whispering, "Joy to the World" for fear of offending the anti-carolers in the neighborhood? Of course, we shouldn't intentionally upset those who don't celebrate Christmas, but we can absolutely still respect those boundaries without muffling our joy or diluting the good news.

Imagine your favorite family member coming from very far away to spend Christmas with you. Would you try to keep it a secret? Or would you tell everyone about your exciting news, post photos of you and your loved one on social media, and maybe even invite friends and extended family over to visit with your favorite person? If you would do all of those things in the excitement of a family member traveling across the country, how much more excitement should we feel over the celebration of Jesus coming all the way from Heaven to spend time with us on earth?

Don't celebrate the arrival of Christ silently, afraid of what others might think. Like Christmas carolers, be unashamed in your celebration! Share your joy with everyone! Shout it from the rooftops. Go tell it on the mountain! You get the idea…

It's impossible to carol alone.

Caroling works best when you're surrounded by other people singing with you. And even if you did go caroling by yourself, you would still need someone to sing to, right?

This is the joy of gathering with friends and family during the Christmas season. It's so much sweeter to be with others who are just as eager to observe Christ's arrival into our world and everything it signifies.

You may not have family living nearby, or you may not have any family at all, but don't let that stop you from congregating with people who love Christmas and celebrating the real reason for the season. Find others in your church who might also be alone for the holidays and organize a special gathering. Maybe you could convince them to join you in a night of neighborhood caroling and hot chocolate? Or maybe you could volunteer for the nursing home ministry, taking the gift of song to the local nursing homes? At the very least, join in the Christmas Eve services in your community.

You never get to hear the carolers if you don't answer the door.

In today's world, answering a knock at the door can be a bit scary, depending on where you live. (My sister recently put in a video doorbell so she can check the live camera feed to see who is at the door.) Or if you work at home like I do, you might not be presentable to answer a knock at the door. (Come on, you've worked at home in your jammies before too!)

Now there's nothing wrong with being a little cautious or introverted when it comes to answering your front door. But how do you respond when Jesus comes knocking on your heart's door? Are you too scared to answer? Or do you feel you're not presentable enough to answer His knock? Or are you simply too busy to be bothered?

If you don't answer your front door this Christmas season, you might miss out on some wonderful Christmas carolers. But if you don't listen for and answer

According to the Merriam-Webster dictionary, the original meaning of the word carol" is "an old round dance with singing." The first known use of the word was way back in the fourteenth century!

The practice has a few possible origins. Some attribute the tradition to the medieval tradition of "wassailing," during which British farmers would drink a toast to their harvest and go door-to-door offering warm cider, well wishes, and an occasional song. According to others, song and dance were common ways to celebrate the winter solstice, and this practice was adapted by Christians as they began celebrating the birth of Christ in the wintertime.[32]

My favorite Christmas carol is "Silent Night"... what's yours?

the knocks on your heart, you might miss out on something far more precious.

Let this season's carolers remind you to boldly share your Christmas joy, gather with others who love Christmas and might feel alone, and answer those all-important door knocks.

And if you're feeling really jolly, gather some family and friends, bundle up, and take to the streets for some good old-fashioned Christmas caroling!

Hearth to Heaven

"Father God, I'm so excited to celebrate the day Heaven came down to earth through Your Son. I don't want to hide that joy. I want to share it with all of my family and friends. I want to share it with You. If You have a message for me in this season, I open my heart to receive it. Amen."

A GIFT FROM GOD

"When they had seen him, they spread the word concerning what had been told them about this child, and all who heard it were amazed at what the shepherds said to them."

LUKE 2:17–18, NIV

By Plane, by Train, by Automobile, or by Foot

By Andy Clapp

Christmas calls us to come back home.

After college, I moved a few hours away from where I grew up. Though the distance was easily overcome, rarely did I drive back home. Work kept me busy. Free time meant I could drive east to spend time with friends from college. I built a new life but even in the middle of the new, there was a deep love for the old.

When Christmas drew near, my heart longed to go home. Each year, I set my sights on Liberty, North Carolina, the little town where my big dreams were born. Family gatherings bring together those I hadn't seen in a year. The drive up sends me through different towns aglow for the season.

But the highlight is when Liberty comes into view. My excitement grows as I make the turn left just past the library. My heart is home.

There's just something about the place. It's where I'm meant to be. Down on Greensboro Street stands the enormous town Christmas tree. I always pull over to take in the sight of the tree in the silence of the night. The decorated storefronts lead to a walk down Swannanoa Avenue, with a short trip down Fayetteville Street to see the

Liberty Showcase Theatre and other stores. For over one hundred years, my family has called Liberty home. When I arrive back to the small town, my soul finds its haven.

Life carries us into different places.

College takes many away from home, beginning a life journey into different areas. Careers relocate our residence. Travel pulls us to see what other places have to offer. Yet Christmas always redirects us back home.

The first Christmas called a young couple back to the land of their fathers. Though Caesar called for a census, it was planned out hundreds of years earlier. God destined that this young couple be in Bethlehem on that night.

The journey no doubt was a struggle. The difficulties of traveling during those times combined with Mary's pregnant condition presented a great challenge. Such a travel was taxing on them and when they arrived in Bethlehem, they had nowhere to go.

What added to the frustration was the travel was not a choice. Caesar demanded the people be counted. His timing came as the moments drew near for Jesus to come. And so, they went. Luke explained, *"And Joseph also went up from the town of Nazareth in Galilee, to Judea, to the city of David, which is called Bethlehem, because he was of the house and family line of David, to be registered*

The amazing part of Christmas is that we finally make time for people we haven't had a chance to see during the year. We set dates with families and friends to share in the moment and in the spirit of the season. According to AAA, an estimate of over 109 million people were expected to drive more than fifty miles for family gatherings for Christmas 2021.[33]

along with Mary, who was engaged to him and was pregnant" (Luke 2:4-5, HCSB). They traveled back to Joseph's roots.

Their travel plans were not their own. Honestly, they weren't even a result of Caesar's decree. God arranged their travel plans long before either one was born. The reason for them to travel to Bethlehem far surpassed being counted. Prophesy's fulfillment happened when they went from Nazareth to Bethlehem. God had a purpose for those moments in that very place.

Each of us will embark on travels during this holiday season. We assume these dates are dictated by the traditions we hold so dear. Perhaps we've moved away and we will head on a trip back home. Maybe we have a shorter journey to go across town to be with relatives or friends. Is this just another trip? Is it only for the purpose of fulfilling another holiday tradition? What if there is a deeper meaning to it?

Bethlehem was the place for Jesus to be born. Likewise, where He sends you this season holds a purpose. Your kindness may save a life and give value to someone. Your ear may be the one that listens to a voice that never felt heard before.

God planned your position with a purpose, where you go this Christmas, take Him with you. He allows for us to be where we are but there is always a purpose for that place. Forgiveness may need to be extended; guidance may be necessary. Encouragement could come from the words you speak, and hope may come from the story of the Lord's work in your life.

And as you travel, remember the journey of Mary and Joseph. Remember how God led them to Bethlehem at the right moment for a major purpose.

Hearth to Heaven

"Heavenly Father, as we are traveling, give us an even deeper understanding of using the time for Your glory. May You show up in such a way that we look back to remember when You sent us on that particular journey. Keep fresh in our minds that every single interaction has a purpose. In Jesus' name we pray, Amen."

A GIFT FROM GOD

"And Joseph also went up from the town of Nazareth in Galilee, to Judea, to the city of David, which is called Bethlehem, because he was of the house and family line of David, to be registered along with Mary, who was engaged to him and was pregnant."

LUKE 2:4-5, HCSB

Every Kind of Cookie

By Michelle Medlock Adams

Have you ever been to a Christmas cookie swap? Talk about fun! (Good friends and lots of carbs…what could be better, right?) In case you're not familiar with cookie swaps, here's how they work: Everybody bakes a batch of their favorite Christmas cookies and brings them to the party. Once everyone arrives, the cookies are divided amongst the guests, and everyone gets to go home with a sampling of all the homemade treats. It's the best night ever with sprinkles on top!

My favorite part of a cookie swap? Trying so many different kinds of cookies. We often settle into an annual rhythm, choosing from the same set of recipes year after year. But at the cookie swap, you're introduced to new kinds of cookies, possibly ones that you would never try otherwise. (Trust me, you'll be asking all of your friends for their recipes!)

Plus, many of the cookies come with their own stories. A German *pfeffernüsse* recipe passed down for five generations. Gluten-free peppermint cookies from the mother of a child with special dietary needs. Gingerbread men decorated like *Star Wars* characters from a sci-fi fanatic. The cookies often say so much about the person who baked them. (To add a bit more fun to the cookie swap, don't label your cookies and let everyone try and figure out which guest brought which cookies.)

The beauty of the cookie swap is that everyone brings something different to the table—their own histories, their own talents, and their own passions. For me, that's the heart of it. (Although I am a huge fan of the cookie-munching, too!) There's something so special about taking the time to make something that's uniquely "you" for the people you love. It's like sharing a piece of your heart.

Now, listen, even if you're not "Betty Crocker" who can ice cookies that look better than a New York bakery's delectables—don't worry. It's easy to fall into the old comparison trap this time of year, and I'm not just talking about cookie swap comparisons. You know what I'm talking about… you look around and see other people celebrating Christmas the way it's "supposed" to be done and feel like you don't measure up. Maybe it's a friend who offers wonderful hospitality this time of year, but you can't imagine inviting people into your own home full of toys and messes. Maybe it's someone at church who's delivering toys to families in need, but the thought of talking with strangers makes your stomach nervous. Maybe it's the person organizing the Christmas party *and* the children's pageant *and* the church mailers, but you feel like you can barely organize your own household.

If you're feeling that way today, let me encourage you. You don't need to be good at everything. In fact, you weren't created to be good at everything. As members of the Body of Christ, we are called to do different tasks. We all have different callings. The same way our gifts and our experiences cause us to bring different cookies to the cookie swap, our gifts and experiences equip us to bring different abilities and offerings to the Kingdom of God.

Just look at the different skills needed to make various types of cookies. For example, making merengues takes careful attention to get the egg consistency just right. Oatmeal cookies require strong muscles to mix the dense dough. Sugar twists take steady hands and precise movements.

In the same way, our spiritual gifts and callings require a specific skill set. Making guests feel welcome takes a giftedness in hospitality. Serving people face-to-face takes an ability to approach new people. Managing "all the things" requires organizational and leadership skills. God created each one of us with unique abilities and giftings so that we can fulfill the calling He has for us! Of course, sometimes God calls us to positions or roles that feel overwhelming, but don't panic. He will always give you what you need. He created you with great care, and He has blessed you with your own special set of talents.

One of the earliest (and most famous) cookie swaps is the Wellesley Cookie Exchange. They even have their own cookbook.[34]

The Exchange was started in 1969 by Mary Bevilacqua and Laurel Gabel, two neighbors who wanted to bring their loved ones together for a time to connect and relax. When their guests finished chatting over dinner, they rang a bell to signal the main event: swapping their cookies! Each guest passed their cookies around, sharing the stories behind their recipes.

Today, Mary's daughters Kristen and Ann continue the legacy of the Cookie Exchange. I can't imagine a more fun (and tasty) family tradition!

This season, I want to encourage you to figure out what you can do uniquely well and how you can serve the Lord this Christmas and throughout the coming year. Seek opportunities in your community to use your talents for the glory of God and celebrate those around you who have their own unique gifts. And while you're at it…invite some friends over for a cookie swap! I'll bring the sprinkles…

Hearth to Heaven

"Lord, please show me how I can serve You and Your people this Christmas season. Use the talents You've so graciously gifted me to bless those around me. Amen."

A GIFT FROM GOD

"Each of you should use whatever gift you have received to serve others,
as faithful stewards of God's grace in its various forms."

1 PETER 4:10, NIV

Red Kettles and Bells Ringing

By Andy Clapp

Bells ring throughout cities across America.

Volunteers decked out in Santa hats ring bells during the Christmas season. The humble chime tells passersby that an opportunity awaits. Before them is a chance to give and bless someone in need. Braving the cold and the elements, the bells sing during Christmas time.

A Christmas without the Salvation Army's presence wouldn't be Christmas at all.

The Salvation Army's work transforms lives today as it has since William Booth began the ministry in 1865. Rather than follow the traditional church model, Booth took to the streets to reach the lost with the gospel. He also trained other evangelists as they saw the streets as the mission field. Booth and others went to those who'd most likely never enter a church.[35]

Nearly one thousand of these trained leaders led many others to Christ. Among some of the first reached were the thieves, drunkards, and prostitutes. Those who found Jesus began to preach themselves, leading others to the One who had changed their lives. The Army grew and it reached those beyond the scope of traditional ministries.

Booth's vision met criticism. The criticism, however, didn't stop him or those committed to the cause. Now, over 150 years later, the Salvation Army continues to do great work. Their presence at Christmas is so important. The donations they receive are absolutely necessary. Through the generosity of shoppers during the Christmas season, the Salvation Army provides nights of shelter to those who have nowhere to go. Meals are financed through donations to feed the ones who have nothing to eat. The ministry serves the neglected and the overlooked.

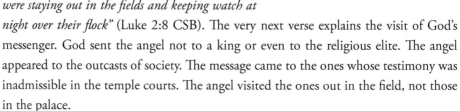

The drive and the desire of the Salvation Army mirrors an incredible truth of the first Christmas. While most would expect the most prominent to hear the news first, the truth of the Bible tells us that God's plan looked far different from man's expectation.

Luke records, *"In the same region, shepherds were staying out in the fields and keeping watch at night over their flock"* (Luke 2:8 CSB). The very next verse explains the visit of God's messenger. God sent the angel not to a king or even to the religious elite. The angel appeared to the outcasts of society. The message came to the ones whose testimony was inadmissible in the temple courts. The angel visited the ones out in the field, not those in the palace.

The Bible says these outcasts hurried after they received the invitation from above. Included for once, they raced to see the Messiah, to behold the glory of the Son of God. No longer on the outside, God Himself called out to them, beckoning them to come.

God's reach to the shepherds in the fields reassures each of us. We do not have to be rich, influential, or powerful. His arms extend to us in the same manner as they did to the shepherds. He sees us as worthy to see, worthy to hear, and worth saving.

The Salvation Army saw the overlooked, the struggling, those considered outcasts. William Booth witnessed those on the streets as worth reaching out to even as others passed by without blinking an eye. Rather than waiting for the outcasts to come to church, Booth and his army took the church to them. In essence, they tried to replicate what they saw in Christmas. Rather than wait, God sent His Son to the world and approached the outcasts.

The ringing of the bell makes a huge impact. In the 2020 holiday season, the Salvation Army raised $557 million, according to the *Washington Times*.[36]

So much can be learned and reflected upon as we hear the bells of the Salvation Army ring this Christmas. For one, we have a chance to give from the surplus of our lives in order to positively impact those in need. Secondly, the sound of the bells challenges us to see the overlooked around us.

Christmas provides the opportunity to share the gospel with the backdrop of Jesus all around us. But instead of waiting on people to come to us, let's go to where they are. Let's share with the ones no one else seems to notice. Let's give to others what the Lord has given to us—hope, value, the way to salvation, and new life.

Hearth to Heaven

"Heavenly Father, give us the heart to reach those unreached before. May we have a passion and dedication like William Booth and all those who have served in the Salvation Army. Send us out into the fields just as You sent the angels to the shepherds out in the field."

A Gift from God

"Then an angel of the Lord stood before them, and the glory of the Lord shone around them, and they were terrified."

LUKE 2:9, CSB

Be Joyful Like Buddy!

By Michelle Medlock Adams

I live for that first day of November every year because that's the day we officially kick off "the holiday season" at the Adams household. I begin watching holiday movies, playing Christmas music, shopping for presents, and decorating our home. Now, I realize my holiday enthusiasm isn't shared by everyone—at least not until about mid-December—and that's okay. (I'll try not to annoy you too much until you get your holiday spirit on.) But honestly, I can't help it. I absolutely love Christmas! And it's not just because it involves presents and fudge, though those perks are worth noting.

I guess that I'm a little like Buddy from that iconic Christmas movie, *Elf*. Remember him? He was so full of childlike wonder and joy. Christmas does that for a lot of us. But "a lot of us" isn't everyone, so I realize there are people whose joy level is low this time of year—maybe because it's the first holiday season without a loved one, or because money is very tight, or simply because it's getting colder, and the days are getting shorter.

No matter the reason, if your joy level is a little low today, I know how we can increase it, using the letters from JOY.

J: Center your life on **Jesus**—See, you can't experience true joy unless you have totally given your life to Christ, allowing Him to empty you out so He can fill you up. What does centering your life on Jesus mean? It means making Him the focus of your entire life. It means waking up thinking about Him and going to bed thinking about Him. If you'll keep Jesus first place in your life, you'll never have a deficit of joy in your heart.

Matthew 6:33 says, *"But seek first the kingdom of God and his righteousness, and all these things will be added to you"* (ESV). Seek Jesus first, and the joy will follow. In other words, if you've lost your joy, don't seek joy; seek the Joy Giver.

O: Overflow in love—When you let God's love fill you up so much that you overflow with His love onto others, joy is sure to follow. You may be thinking, "That sounds great, Michelle, but how do I do that?" Start each day by reading First Corinthians 13—the Love Chapter—and ask the Lord to give you opportunities throughout the day to share His love with everyone you encounter.

And here's another "o" word that goes right along with overflowing in love—**others**. Be others-minded as you go through life. Matthew 7:12, also known as the Golden Rule, instructs us to: *"Do to others whatever you would like them to do to you"* (NLT).

You might pay for the person's order in the car behind you when you're grabbing your morning coffee and breakfast sandwich. Or maybe you could start an outreach program at your church where you visit the shut-ins and possibly take them groceries or simply share a cup of tea and pray with them. Or maybe you could offer to do a few household tasks for that nice elderly couple in your neighborhood. Look for ways to bless others, and that joy you've been missing will return.

Y: You need to look forward—In order to experience joy and walk in it this season, you're going to have to put the past in the past at last. In other words, don't dwell on the past—look to the future. I realize it's the end of another year, and you may not have accomplished all that you'd hoped, or you may have experienced loss or hurt this year but leave all of that behind as we get ready to enter into a New Year.

Have you ever wondered why the windshield in your car is so large and the rearview mirror is so small? It's because what's behind you—what has happened in your past—isn't nearly as important as what is in your future. Proverbs 4:25 (ESV) says, *"Let your eyes look directly forward, and your gaze be straight before you."*

Keep gazing ahead to all that God has for you! That's sure to bring joy to your heart! But if you're too busy looking behind, replaying all of the times you failed God or missed an opportunity, your joy tank is going to be empty. Here's the thing, if you've asked Jesus to forgive your past sins, He doesn't even remember them anymore, so why should you? Remember, the Word tells us that God's mercies are new every morning. There's a reason for that—He knew we'd need new mercies every day. He loves you unconditionally, and that fact alone should put joy in your heart.

Since I mentioned *Elf* in this devotion, I thought it might be fun to feature five little-known facts about this beloved Christmas movie.

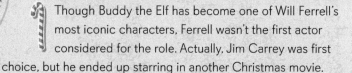

Though Buddy the Elf has become one of Will Ferrell's most iconic characters, Ferrell wasn't the first actor considered for the role. Actually, Jim Carrey was first choice, but he ended up starring in another Christmas movie.

 The director of *Elf*, Jon Favreau, usually makes an appearance in the films he directs. *Elf* was no exception. He played Buddy's doctor in *Elf*. He also voiced the rabid raccoon that Buddy encounters.

 In 2006, Ferrell admitted in an interview that he turned down $29 million to star in an *Elf* sequel because he just didn't want to do it for the money. "I remember asking myself: could I withstand the criticism when it's bad and they say, 'He did the sequel for the money?' I decided I wouldn't be able to."

 Remember Buddy's ridiculously long burp after drinking a 2-liter of Coke? Though uncredited, that lengthy belch came from voice actor Maurice LaMarche, who might be best known for being the voice of Brain in *Pinky and the Brain*.[37]

 In the scene where Buddy is testing the jack-in-the-box toys, Ferrell is not acting when you see that fear on his face when the jack pops out of the box. Apparently, Favreau used remote control devices to make them randomly go off so he could get authentic reactions from Buddy. It worked![38]

Hearth to Heaven

"Father, I know that Your joy is the source of my strength, so I am asking You to infuse Your joy into me so that I might share it with others who might also need a joy boost this season. And, Father, help me to center my life on You, overflow with Your love, and look forward to all that You have for me. Help me, Lord, to forget the past. I praise You, God, for Your mercies that are new every morning. I love You, Lord. In the Mighty Name of Your Son, Jesus, Amen."

A GIFT FROM GOD

"May the God of hope fill you with all joy and peace as you trust in him, so that you may overflow with hope by the power of the Holy Spirit."

ROMANS 15:13, NIV

Mary, Joseph, and the Baby, Together in a Stable

By Andy Clapp

What stands as a reminder of the real meaning of the season?

One of the most touching aspects of Christmas is the nativity scene. Featured on Christmas cards sent around the world, the image takes us to the heart of Christmas. Across the nation, churches host live nativity scenes. Cars filled with eager viewers pull through to see angels perched outside the stable, Mary and Joseph, and the newborn who gives us a reason to celebrate. Families display the scene on tabletops and on the mantle. Ornaments hang with the outline of that night in Bethlehem.

Our nativity scenes never return to a box. Displayed throughout the year, my wife Crystal's Willow Tree set remains on the mantle.

"I love my nativity," she expresses from time to time.

Her eyes shift upwards to see the display again. We never move it. The reason is clear. When life is hard, the nativity scene reminds us that we have a reason to celebrate. He came. When we feel worried, we are reminded that the Prince of Peace entered the world in a stable.

The other nativity scene is featured on a lantern given to us one Christmas by our best friends. The light inside draws the eyes to see the beauty of the scene before us. I often stare at the lantern as it brings such a peace and a great perspective to all that life throws at us. The glow reminds me that all is well in my soul even when all is not well within the world.

The presence of the nativity scene keeps our focus on Christ during the season. A nativity scene in Spain cannot be overlooked due to its soaring heights. As of 2020, the largest nativity scene in the world is located in Alicante, Spain. The statue of Joseph stands an incredible fifty-nine feet tall.[39]

These depictions, whether live, wooden, or chiseled into a lantern, take us to the heart of a lifelong celebration. The season of Christmas reinforces the reason for joy, but that joy is to be carried throughout the year. His coming didn't spark euphoria for a day, but instead sets the soul ablaze forever.

Commercialism pulls us to focus on the gifts we will give. Toy companies reveal the hottest toys of the year. Car companies implore us to show love through the purchase of a new vehicle while jewelers persuade us to buy jewelry. A barrage of advertising turns us to the commercial side of the season. That fact makes the nativity scene even more important. The outline of the night in Bethlehem refocuses us away from what we will give and back to the place of recognizing what we've been given.

Isaiah's prophecy points us to the miracle. So often, the words of Isaiah are printed with the outline of the nativity. The prophet said, *"For a child will be born for us, a son will be given to us, and the government will be on His shoulders. He will be named Wonderful Counselor, Mighty God, Eternal Father, Prince of Peace"* (Isaiah 9:6, HCSB). For

Isaiah, it was all about the Baby being born that night. No other occurrence mattered as much as the coming of Christ.

When Jesus came, the focus of Mary, Joseph, the angels, the shepherds, and later, the Wise Men, turned to Him. The heart of worship, the source of joy, the thrill of their hearts lay in a manger. A gift from above descended to where they were and just the sight of Him calmed their souls.

Perhaps we need the nativity scene now more than ever before. As we have drifted further away from the heart of Christmas, the representation of the nativity draws us back to where we find all we need. The lure of the world never fulfills in the way that the manger promises.

The nativity scene is a decoration that serves a distinct purpose. While everything else clouds our vision, a depiction of Bethlehem brings joy into clear view. Of all that is packed away after the season, the nativity scene is one that can remain unpacked all year.

The very presence of something that proclaims the birth of hope comforts us throughout the year. It reminds us that His love for us runs deep. We reflect on how in the midst of the seemingly meaningless noise of the world, there is purpose.

Keep the manger in sight so you can be strengthened by what it means every day of the year. The Son of God came to the earth—hope is alive!

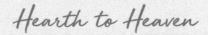

Hearth to Heaven

"Heavenly Father, thank You for the meaning of Christmas, the truth of what took place in Bethlehem. Let us be strengthened by the nativity throughout the year. The fact that Jesus came gives us hope, provides us with joy, and offers us peace even when life is in an uproar. Thank You for the reminders You give to us. In Jesus' name we pray, Amen."

A GIFT FROM GOD

"Then she gave birth to her firstborn Son, and she wrapped Him snugly in cloth and laid Him in a feeding trough—because there was no room for them at the lodging place."

LUKE 2:7, HCSB

Have a Silly, Dilly Christmas

By Michelle Medlock Adams

Have you ever heard of the tradition of the Christmas pickle?

No, really! (I promise I'm not making it up.) Many people hide a pickle-shaped ornament on their Christmas tree, and the first family member to find it on Christmas morning gets a reward! It might be a special prize, the privilege of opening the first gift, or just the promise of good fortune in the year to come. If you've never tried it, you really should. It's a lot harder than it sounds. Because the green pickle blends in so well amid the branches of the evergreen tree, it sometimes takes quite a while to locate!

Why on earth did this become a tradition? Well, some have said it started after the Civil War due to an imprisoned, starving soldier begging a guard for a pickle to eat on Christmas Eve, and crediting his survival to the generous guard and the pickle he provided. Others have said it commemorates a story of Saint Nicholas rescuing two children who were trapped in pickle barrels. The most common belief, however, is that hiding the Christmas pickle is an old German custom that was passed down through generations.[40]

But the funny thing is, a 2016 study showed that ninety-one percent of the Germans surveyed said they'd never heard of the Christmas pickle. So where did it come from?[41]

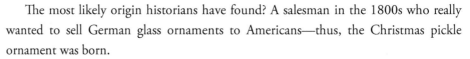

The most likely origin historians have found? A salesman in the 1800s who really wanted to sell German glass ornaments to Americans—thus, the Christmas pickle ornament was born.

Not a precious tradition. Not a heartwarming tale of generosity. Just a guy who wanted people to give him their money.

This seems a bit silly now. Why would people fall for the marketing of something as ridiculous as a Christmas pickle ornament? But honestly, I don't think we're all that different from the first people who bought those glass Christmas pickle ornaments.

Seriously, how many holiday hoops do we jump through each year, all because it "just wouldn't be Christmas without it?" We put so much pressure on ourselves to do everything we're "supposed" to do for Christmas, that we can lose the joy and wonder of the season. Does the Bible say we must celebrate Christ's birth by baking a dozen of every type of Christmas cookie? Will we grow closer in our relationship with Jesus because we made sure to buy a new commemorative ornament for every family member this year? Do we gain more grace if we put up a Christmas tree the day after Thanksgiving and make sure it's packed away by January 1?

In reality, we do these things because we feel like we will be letting everyone down if we don't continue in the craziness. We mistakenly listen to "the pickle ornament salesmen" in our lives and believe that he knows what we need. Maybe your pickle salesman looks like an online article advertising a certain toy that will be under *every* tree this year, implying that your child will be missing out if one of those isn't under *your* tree. Or maybe your pickle salesman is a magazine-worthy photo on social media that makes you wonder if you should swap out all of your sentimental, not-very-aesthetically-pleasing decorations for minimalist neutrals or rustic farmhouse decor.

I want to encourage you to take a moment to think about what's most important during this season: celebrating the birth of Jesus with the people you love most. Anything that doesn't contribute to that pursuit can be set aside—without any guilt.

What have you been told that you need to buy, do, or keep track of that are just distractions from the heart of Christmas? What lies have you believed that were nothing more than marketing ploys from "a salesman?"

There's nothing wrong with fun, family holiday traditions. Like decorating the tree together while watching holiday movies, wearing matching Christmas pjs, or even searching for the well-hidden pickle in the branches of your Christmas tree. If your traditions bring your family together for a time of memory-making and festive fun...that's wonderful! But as you fill up your calendar and add more things to your Christmas to-do list, pause and praise God for the real reason we celebrate Christmas, and maybe purchase a glass Christmas pickle as a visual reminder.

If you're a fan of the Christmas pickle, take a trip to Berrien Springs, Michigan! The small town has been named the "Christmas Pickle Capital of the World," and it's the home of the annual Pickle Festival. The festival's activities include pickle decorating, a pickle toss, and an ice cream social. According to the Berrien Springs website, the festival is "an event to relish." You might say it's kind of a big dill![42]

Hearth to Heaven

"Father God, there is so much going on in this season. But what's most important to me throughout all of the festivities is remembering that You sent Your Son to earth all those years ago to live among us. When I get distracted by the to-do lists and advertisements, Lord, I ask You to refocus my heart on Jesus. Amen."

A GIFT FROM GOD

"[B]ut the worries of this life, the deceitfulness of wealth and the desires for other things come in and choke the word, making it unfruitful."

MARK 4:19, NIV

Setting the Mood for the Season

By Andy Clapp

Do you hear what I am hearing?

The sounds of the season fill the air as the Yule Log crackles on the television. The screen shows a roaring fireplace and no matter where you are, the Yule Log soothes every soul. Sinatra, Bing Crosby, and others accent the celebration. Our family opens gifts on Christmas morning in front of the broadcasted fire.

Years ago, my schedule demanded that I work on Christmas Eve. At the time, I worked the front desk at a hotel, so my turn came to work the third shift on a holiday. My heart longed to be with my family, but work insisted I fulfill my eight hours. With no one in sight and the rest of the world asleep, I discovered the Yule Log playing on the television in the lobby. I sat at one of the tables and wrote a few pages in a Christmas novel I was working on. Certain mainstays bring Christmas to wherever you are.

Eight hours passed faster than ever before as I lost myself in the moment.

I could hear the songs proclaim the good news of Christmas's arrival. I heard, in my place of desperation, the songs that spoke of hope eternal.

The origination of the televised-fireplace phenomenon began with a TV executive in New York City. Rather than stick to the schedule, Fred Thrower proposed a change. A seventeen-second loop of a fireplace, with music in the background, laid the foundation for a new tradition. WPIX-TV created a staple of the season that spread to other channels. What started as a three-hour special grew to a twenty-four-hour marathon today.

For those who cannot get enough, Yule Log DVDs offer buyers a chance to experience the Yule Log anytime during the year. As Christmas features such special music, the fireplace visual and holiday audio speak to the soul.

The Yule Log changes the environment of a place. What you see, what you hear, draws you into that Christmas state of being whether it is a snowy night in December or a warm summer's night in July.

During the original filming of the Yule Log, the footage was taken at Gracie Mansion. However, during the filming, sparks escaped and burned up a $4,000 rug. When the time came to shoot new footage, the film crews had to choose a different location.[43]

Much of the Christmas euphoria is in the atmosphere. The Yule Log completes that atmosphere. It looks like Christmas. It sounds like Christmas.

As we think about the melody of the season, we reflect on what might have been on the night Jesus was born. The sound that filled the air in Bethlehem was the sound of praise. Angels filled the sky, as far as the eyes could see. A multitude sang the most glorious tune to the most unusual audience—a group of shepherds out in the field. The song spoke of the glory of the Lord. They praised, *"Glory to God in the highest heaven, and peace on earth to people He favors!*" (Luke 2:14 HCSB). Hope's proclamation rang in the ears of the weary shepherds.

Can you imagine that night? The shepherd's plan for the evening was interrupted. At once, the entire atmosphere shifted. What they discussed before no longer mattered. Any prior worries gave way to a focus on angels and a newborn. The supernatural overwhelmed all else. The hillside,

normally ordinary, stood under the canopy of the extraordinary.

What makes Christmas so special? No other holiday celebration brings such a transformation. Decorations are everywhere. Seasonal music rings out in stores and on the radio in the car. Everywhere we turn, we see Christmas. Being immersed in the season enhances the experience.

Just as the Yule Log adds to the festiveness, we look to see how we can alter the atmosphere of our lives throughout the Christmas season and beyond. As we try so hard to complete the Christmas experience, we can strive to maintain a God-filled atmosphere at all times in life.

We control what dominates our atmosphere. We choose the movies we watch. We select the music we play. Much of the environment around us alters with our personal choices. Do we want to be engulfed in worldliness or godliness?

The soul finds peace when the atmosphere of our lives is fixated on the Lord. When we hear of His promises, peace floods our souls. In an atmosphere centered on holiness, we feel His presence and His nearness fills us up where worldliness once emptied us out.

Hearth to Heaven

"Heavenly Father, we ask that You flood our lives with the Holy Spirit this Christmas and every day beyond. We commit to filling the air with praises to Your name. Take over the atmosphere of our lives. We long to be surrounded by You every moment. We need to feel Your presence every day of our lives. In Jesus' name we pray, Amen."

A GIFT FROM GOD

"Glory to God in the highest heaven, and peace on earth to people He favors!"

LUKE 2:14, HCSB

Love Letters for Christmas

By Michelle Medlock Adams

I remember one Christmas when money was so tight, my husband and I opted not to buy each other any gifts. Both of our girls were attending out-of-state colleges, and we had used all of our funds to pay their winter tuition bills. Buying gifts just wasn't in the budget. Still, it felt kind of sad not to give each other any presents, so we decided to write one another heartfelt letters. Because I'm a writer, this was an easy task for me, but for my CPA husband, this was a real labor of love…and that's one of the reasons it meant so much.

I still have his two-page letter, written on yellow notebook paper, tucked safely in the pages of my Bible. Though his handwriting is hardly beautiful—he even scratched out some words and wrote other words above them—I loved every word and every scribble. Why? Because they were precious words, sweet memories, and heartfelt confessions from my favorite person in the world. It's one of the nicest gifts that anyone has ever given me. I even take it out and read that letter from time to time. It's a reminder of how much my husband loves me.

You may not have money for gifts this year, and you may not even have a spouse to write you a love letter. But don't be sad, because you *do* have a Heavenly Father who loves you with an everlasting love, and His Word, the Bible, is filled with precious promises, words of wisdom, and timely encouragement—just for you! The Bible is the ultimate love letter. In its pages, God tells us how much He loves us and all that He has done to demonstrate that love. You'll also discover directives on how to live because God knows what is best for us, and He wants us to walk in all that He has for us. Page after page is filled with promise after promise. So, give yourself a gift this year—start reading your Bible every day. Meditate on its promises, and let God speak to you through its pages. It's the best gift you could ever give yourself.

Though you normally read a book from beginning to end, that's not necessarily the best way to read the Bible. Most people recommend starting in the New Testament, specifically with the four Gospels— Matthew, Mark, Luke, and John. Also, it's a good idea to read a chapter or two in Proverbs and Psalms along with your daily reading in the New Testament.

But that's just one directive. You'll find many available Bible reading plans online. And here are a few more tips for enjoying God's Word.

1 Find an easy-to-read version of the Bible. While some people only read the King James Version, I like to have several different versions at my fingertips. When I'm studying or researching, I like to use the

Amplified Version, but when I'm just reading, I prefer the New International Version or the New Living Translation. And my new favorite? The Passion Translation! (Check out the YouVersion Bible app.)

2. Don't worry if you can't spend hours reading the Bible every day. Start small—maybe five or ten minutes each morning. Spending some time in God's Word is better than no time at all. Try getting up a little earlier  each day and setting aside that time for Bible reading, or maybe use your lunch break at work to meditate on a few scriptures or make reading the Bible the last part of your nighttime routine. Find what works best for you, and then just be consistent with your plan.

3. Before you start reading, ask God to help you understand His Word, and pray that He uses His Word to speak to you. Jeremiah 29:13 (ESV) says, *"You will seek me and find me, when you seek me with all your heart."* So go ahead. Seek Him!

Hearth to Heaven

"Father God, help me to love Your Word like You do, and help me to understand all that You have put in its pages. I love You. Amen."

A GIFT FROM GOD

"Your word is a lamp for my feet, a light on my path."

PSALMS 119:105, NIV

Day 37

He's On His Way

By Andy Clapp

A television news report tells the last known location for Santa and his team of flying reindeer.

NORAD (North American Aerospace Defense Command) tackles the job of notifying the public each Christmas Eve. Informing children of his location ensures the little ones are fast asleep before Santa arrives at their homes. Local television reporters provide updates.

As a child, these "breaking news" features demanded my attention. We spent each Christmas Eve with our family at my grandparents' house. After dinner, we opened our gifts, then played in the living room as the television gave hourly updates on Santa's location.

Around 9 PM, the update came.

"Kids, Santa is getting closer. It is time to get to bed now," the news anchor said. Never before did we care what was said on the news…until those words were uttered.

We panicked. Our parents, still gathered in the other room, faced an onslaught of children desperate to get to bed…the only night of the year we had such a desire.

"Mom, we have to go…"

She tried to continue her conversation.

"We have to get to bed. They said Santa is almost here on TV."

Minutes passed as fear rose in my throat. My mind filled with images of Santa passing by, a Christmas morning devoid of the treasures I longed to find.

After much insistence, we made our way home from my grandparents' house. I rushed upstairs, brushed my teeth, launched myself into the bed, and closed my eyes. NORAD said he was near. I forced my eyes shut in case he was in the neighborhood.

The next morning, I rushed downstairs to see all my heart longed to behold. I was thankful for the advanced warning of NORAD and our local news.

In 2017, NORAD experienced increased call volumes for the season. Volunteers answered over 126,000 calls inquiring about Santa's whereabouts.[44]

We didn't want to be left out. We couldn't miss the opportunity to be amazed the next morning.

What if everything in life had advanced warning?

The coming of Christ did. Isaiah prophesied who Jesus would be and even parts of how He would come into the world. Isaiah foretold, *"The virgin will conceive, have a son, and name Him Immanuel"* (Isaiah 7:14, HCSB). Micah came later and told people where He could come. Micah pointed to Bethlehem, giving the location for people to fix their eyes upon.

Yet most everyone missed it. As Luke recorded the birth of Christ, few stood in attendance. Matthew spoke of visitors who came from the east after traversing rugged terrain. These are the only ones recorded—shepherds and the Wise Men. The rest of the world missed the biggest event, the most noteworthy birth, the very event foretold hundreds of years in advance.

As Christmas comes, all the decorations remind us that something grand awaits during the season. A transformed landscape beckons us to come to the place where God changed the world. But year after year, we miss it. We focus on everything else and miss the beauty of the Lord.

Innkeepers overlooked desperation at their door. A town full of visitors missed the most important visitor in Bethlehem. A world forewarned that the night would come lost sight over time. Life happened. A list of things to do distracted them from the very hope they were desperate to find.

For nearly a month, even an unbelieving world points to something of great significance. We know the significance. We celebrate that Christ came. However, with a list of things to do, gifts to buy, and places to be, we easily stray away from the true meaning. We forget the reason to celebrate as we get caught up in the other facets of Christmas.

Don't miss Him this year. He came to the earth and His coming gives us a reason to celebrate.

The writers of the gospels tell the story the prophets foretold. When we see Him, when we pay attention to the Lord in this season, we awaken Christmas morning to find all we dreamed of. The gifts of hope, joy, grace, mercy, love, and salvation are wrapped in a Baby, a gift sent for us. We were told ahead of time to be on the lookout—did we heed the advanced warning?

He told the world He was coming, and He did! Now, let's keep our eyes open because His word says He's coming again.

Hearth to Heaven

"Heavenly Father, we thank You for sending us Your Son. Open our eyes, our hearts, and our minds so we do not miss Jesus this year. Remind us of the reason. Thank You for advanced warning, and we thank You for Your Word as it prepares us in this special season. In Jesus' name we pray, Amen."

A Gift From God

"Therefore, the Lord Himself will give you a sign: The virgin will conceive, have a son, and name him Immanuel."

ISAIAH 7:14, HCSB

Christmas Pjs, Yay!

By Michelle Medlock Adams

Last October, my friend Angie and I headed to the annual Covered Bridge Festival in Southern Indiana. With both of us being new Gigis, we couldn't wait to buy Christmas presents for our grandkids. And boy, did we have fun! Our favorite stop? A darling little children's boutique that even offered personalization.

It may have only been October, but it sure felt like Christmas as we shopped for matching holiday pajamas for the littles in our world. Both Angie and I chose the bright red flannel jammies with each grandbaby's initials monogrammed right on the front. And the girls' pjs had ruffles on the bum! So cute!

I could hardly wait for Christmas Eve so that I could see all five of my grandkids—from four months to four years old—dressed in those matching pjs. And to my surprise, they loved them! They didn't care that they were darling, or that they were monogramed, or that they were fuzzy-soft flannel. You know what they loved?

That they matched each other!

"We are the same!" Wren beamed, looking down at her jammies and then back at her cousins.

All evening long, the cousin crew played superheroes, running through the house in a blur of red, before finally collapsing on a pile of pillows and blankets to watch *The Grinch*—together.

My grandkiddos adore one another, and they don't get to see each other very often, so we try to make the most of our holidays together. And now our Christmas Eve gathering includes matching jammies.

As I write this devotion, I'm already on the hunt for this year's fam jams. (We're even considering having the adults wear matching jammies too, like so many other families do.)

There's something very special about feeling like you belong and celebrating that family bond—even if you're doing it via flannel pjs. Whether you don them for a holiday movie marathon or save them for Christmas Eve, go ahead and join the matching fam jams craze.

Family is so important, and in today's hurting world, many families are broken, separated, and unhappy. Listen, I'm not implying that matching pajamas will fix your family, but I know what will! Or rather, I know Who will—God.

Your Heavenly Father is big on family, and if you're a Christian, you're a member of His family. You can call on Him day or night, and you can trust Him to put your earthly family back together. So if you have a prodigal child, give that child to Him. Begin praising God every day that your child is protected, and that God is working in your baby's life, bringing your child back to Him and back to you. Pray those things out loud because the Bible tells us, that faith comes by hearing, so you can build your faith regarding your wayward child just by hearing yourself pray.

Maybe you don't have a rebellious child, but some of your family relationships are strained, and you're worried about getting together for the holidays; don't worry—pray. Worry never changed anything but prayer always produces results. Now, those results may not manifest as quickly as we'd like, but just keep on praying, praising, and believing. God is good, and He is able. He is all about restoring families, and when God restores, it's even better than before.

So just how did the phenomena of matching family jammies begin? According to fashion historian Debbie Sessions, matching holiday pjs were popular long before we had Instagram. In fact, they date back to holiday department store catalogs of the 1950s.

But this fun family tradition got a huge boost in popularity in 2013 when the Holderness family from North Carolina made a hilarious music video parody called, "Christmas Jammies" and it went viral on social media. Today, that video has more than eighteen million views, and the hashtag #ChristmasJammies has been used more than 193,000 times by families showing off their fam jams![45]

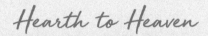

Hearth to Heaven

"Father God, thank you for my family. I pray that You bless our holiday get-togethers, and that You bond us to one another with Your love. I am so thankful that I am part of Your family, God. I love You. Amen."

A GIFT FROM GOD

"But to all who did receive him, who believed in his name, he gave the right to become children of God."

JOHN 1:12, ESV

'Twas the Night Before Christmas

By Andy Clapp

One Christmas tradition unfolds in the final hours.

As my children prepare to go to bed, we gather on the couch for the last tradition before Christmas morning arrives. Decked out in Christmas pajamas, a book draws everyone to gather in close, to share in the moment. We read "A Visit from St. Nicholas" as they look at the pictures and imagine what the next morning will bring. Excitement leads to wiggling. The description of Santa causes giggling.

Inevitably, we face the questions of "how" as we read.

"How does he do it?"

Prepared for such a question ahead of time, we answer without hesitation.

"How old is Santa?"

"Really old," I explained one year.

"Older than you?" my daughter asked. I knew she meant it sincerely, but it revealed how old she thought I was.

"Definitely older than daddy," came the reply.

As the world calms for the night, a moment is shared through a story. Written and published anonymously in 1823, later attributed to Clement Clarke Moore, the poem makes memories two hundred years later. Moore's words fill the air every Christmas, his words some of the most recognizable of the season. Families throughout the world take a few minutes to share in the wonder of his writing.

In 2006, one of the four known handwritten copies of Moore's poem was sold to a private collector. The collector paid $280,000 for the handwritten copy. The copy sold dated back to 1860 and had the signature of Clement Clarke Moore on the copy. The remaining three copies are displayed in museums. One of the copies is displayed in the New York Historical Library.[46]

To further the joy of Moore's poem, we select a night each year to watch the cartoon version. Complete with our Jiffy Pop popcorn, we see Moore's words come alive in the animated story of a clockmaker's family and a family of mice.

The poem, however, pales in comparison to the story we share as dawn breaks the next morning. Before the children open their gifts, again we gather on the couch. A different book sits central before us. On this morning, the words of Luke 2:1-20 fills the air. We travel back to Bethlehem. We reconnect with the reason for the celebration. The words speak hope into all of our lives. Christ's coming gives meaning, not only to the day, but to every day of life.

The greatest story is the story of the birth of Immanuel—"God with us." As the angels shared with the shepherds, the happenings of that night were *"good news of great joy that will be for all the people"* (Luke 2:10, HCSB). A simple opening of the Bible reveals the greatest gift of Christmas. The story sets the stage for more than just a day of celebrating. The story of the birth of Christ fills our hearts with wonder in a way nothing else can.

A new chapter begins with each Christmas. As this year's story is written, take time to include the greatest story. Moore's work has served as a tradition for two hundred years. Luke's gospel has served as the foundation of Christmas for two thousand years.

What makes the story so powerful is that you are the reason He came, we needed Him more than anything else, and He came. He fills our lives with all we need and those words—"good news of great joy"—should be the most recognizable words of this season.

Put the right story at the heart of the celebration every year. We can enjoy a poem about Santa and watch children dream about what will be when the morning sun rises. More important, however, is the story of Bethlehem that invites each of us to come and see what God has done.

Hearth to Heaven

"Dear Lord, give us a passion to go back to the heart of the story every Christmas. Give us a desire to connect with the good news and to share that good news with family and friends. Keep our focus on the reason we celebrate this season. In Jesus' name we pray, Amen."

A GIFT FROM GOD

"Today a Savior, who is Messiah the Lord, was born for you in the city of David."

LUKE 2:11, HCSB

Day 40

No White Elephant Gifts with Jesus

By Michelle Medlock Adams

Our white elephant family get-together on Christmas Eve is something we look forward to all year, and we start shopping for that perfect gag gift on January 1. (I bought my white elephant gift in March—it's the best, lol! I found it at Goodwill and squealed when I put it in the cart, envisioning my sister opening it on December 24. I can hardly wait!) We take our white elephant gift exchange seriously.

Last year, my son-in-law Micah ended up opening my gift—a singing, dancing Christmas tree with big, googly eyes. His exact words when he opened it and turned it on…"Scary. This is truly terrifying," he said. "Thank you so much." I have to admit, it was a little off-putting, which is part of the fun!

I, on the other hand, ended up with the gift my other son-in-law Wesley brought. Wes is a hunter, so his gift to me? Deer urine. Because nothing says "Christmas" like deer urine, right?

Some families buy sweet, nice gifts that anyone could enjoy. Obviously, that's not us. We buy crazy, comical, and always hilarious gifts, and honestly, I thought everyone's white elephant gift exchanges were like ours. I found out the hard way,

177

that's not the case when our women's Bible study group had its first white elephant gift exchange. The only instructions were posted in the church bulletin, "Please bring a gift costing less than $15." I remember thinking, "Wow, you can get a lot at Goodwill for $15!" So, I found a Billy the Bass wall mount that sang, "Take Me to the River," and I wrapped it beautifully. I couldn't wait to engage in a night of hilarity.

But that's not exactly how it played out. As the gift exchange progressed, and people opened their chosen gifts, one by one, I soon realized I might have missed an important piece of information. Apparently, we were supposed to bring a NICE gift that any woman would love, not a gag gift. Woman after woman opened wonderful candles and fuzzy slippers and beautiful Christmas ornaments. I opened an adorable houndstooth-print scarf. And then…I saw a lady go for my present. My heart was pounding so hard and so fast, that I was sure everyone could hear it.

Just play it cool, Michelle. No one will know you're the one who brought Billy the Bass.

She carefully unwrapped it, gave an awkward smile, and held it up for all to see.

"It's a…it's some kind of singing fish, I think," she mumbled.

Dead silence.

Not even a snicker.

I wanted the earth to open up and swallow me, but thankfully, the game moved quickly. We were on to the next gift in just a moment. But that was the longest moment of my life.

I just couldn't let that woman go home with Billy the Bass—not when every other woman had a real gift. I planned to go and "steal" it from her when it was my turn again, insisting that my hubby would love it because of his obsession with bass fishing, but I didn't have to do that after all. Another lady beat me to it, saying, "My grandson will love this! I must have your Billy the Bass!"

Whew! I had escaped without anyone knowing I'd been the idiot who brought a gag gift to a nice white elephant gift exchange, and everyone went home happy.

I was so thankful!

You know what else I'm thankful for today? That when we come to Jesus, it isn't a "luck of the draw" kind of white elephant gift exchange. Instead, it's the best gift exchange ever! We give Him all of our sins, worries, and "junk," and He gives us salvation, freedom, eternal life with Him, peace, love, joy, and so much more! And you know how in most white elephant gift exchanges, there's always one gift that everyone wants because it's the best item? So everyone "fights" over that one gift, stealing it from its current holder, time and time again. It's not like that with God. He has enough of "the best" to go around. You don't have to fight for it. He gives it to us freely. What a deal!

Whether or not you'll be participating in any white elephant gift exchanges this year, I hope you'll participate in this one—give others the gift of Jesus. Share your testimony with your unsaved friends and family if the opportunity presents itself, and if you haven't ever asked Jesus to be the Lord of your life—if you've sort of breezed past the other invitations to do so in this devotional, now is your chance! Just pray,

"Lord, I confess that I've sinned and that I need a savior. I believe that you died on the cross for my sins, and I'm so grateful. I make You the Lord of my life today. I love You. Amen."

The gift of salvation.

Now, that beats any white elephant gift!

Hearth to Heaven

"Lord, please give me the courage to share my faith with others and offer them the greatest gift of all time. I am so thankful for Your gift of salvation. I love you, Lord. Amen."

A GIFT FROM GOD

"For the wages of sin is death, but the gift of God is eternal life in Christ Jesus our Lord."

ROMANS 6:23, NIV

FESTIVE FUN FACTS · FESTIVE FUN FACTS ·

If you've never participated in a white elephant gift exchange, let me give you the basics. It doesn't matter if it's a group of coworkers, family and friends, church folks, or your neighbors—as long as you have a group of people, you can have a white elephant gift exchange. Prior to the gathering, decide (and communicate to everyone) whether the gift will be a nice gift or a gag gift, and set a price range.

Every person brings a nicely wrapped gift with no nametag, and places it in the pile of gifts, usually in the center of the room. Participants then pick a number from a hat, and take turns in numerical order, choosing a gift from the pile—or "stealing" from an earlier participant who has already chosen a present—until everyone has a present in front of them.

The rules can vary a bit, particularly as it relates to how many times a gift can be stolen, but usually, once someone has had possession of a gift three times, it's theirs! In other words, no one can steal that gift again.

White elephant gift exchanges are great fun, especially if the participants have a good sense of humor. Be prepared, though. There always seems to be one or two people who loudly object to the gifts they ended up with at the game's conclusion. And to that, I'll quote my southern friend Eva Diva, "Bless their hearts."

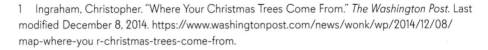

Endnotes

1   Ingraham, Christopher. "Where Your Christmas Trees Come From." *The Washington Post.* Last modified December 8, 2014. https://www.washingtonpost.com/news/wonk/wp/2014/12/08/map-where-you r-christmas-trees-come-from.

2   Rossen, Jake. "8 Festive Facts About Hallmark Channel Christmas Movies," *Mental Floss.* Last modified November 20, 2019, https://www.mentalfloss.com/article/608916/hallmark-channel-christmas-movie-facts.

3   "Who Invented Electric Christmas Lights?" The Library of Congress. Last modified November 19, 2019. https://www.loc.gov/everyday-mysteries/technology/item/who-invented-electric-christmas-lights/.

4   "Stocking Stuffer & Consumer Insight Surprises." Endcaps & Insights | Retail Blog. Accessed November 29, 2022. https://blog.fieldagent.net/stocking-stuffer-and-consumer-insight-surprises.

5   "Home Alone Scene 8," Homework Help & Study Guides For Students | Shmoop. Accessed November 7, 2022, https://www.shmoop.com/study-guides/movie/home-alone/summary/scene-8.

6   Vargas, Chanel. "What We Know About the Rare "Christmas Star" That Formed in 2020, Which We Won't See Again Until 2080!" POPSUGAR Smart Living. Last modified December 2, 2020. https://www.popsugar.com/smart-living/jupiter-saturn-christmas-star-48024008.

7   "A Charlie Brown Christmas." IMDb. Accessed December 3, 2022. https://www.imdb.com/title/tt0059026/.

8 "Just a Moment..." Just a Moment... Accessed August 28, 2022. https://tvshowtranscripts.ourboard.org/viewtopic.php?f=150&t=32381.

9 "How "A Charlie Brown Christmas" Came to Be—and Almost Didn't." Newsweek. Last modified December 8, 2021. https://www.newsweek.com/how-charlie-brown-christmas-came-almost-didnt-1656940.

10 "Elements of a Candle: Wax." National Candle Association. Last modified July 23, 2020. https://candles.org/elements-of-a-candle/wax/.

11 Court, Andrew. "'World's Most Expensive' Advent Calendar is Custom-made for $10M." New York Post. Last modified December 2, 2021. https://nypost.com/2021/12/02/worlds-most-expensive-custom-advent-calendar-costs-10m/.

12 "The 10 Best Quotes In Virgin River (Including Season 4)." ScreenRant. Last modified July 23, 2022. https://screenrant.com/virgin-river-best-quotes-including-season-4/.

13 Wood, Jennifer M. "25 Wonderful Facts About It's a Wonderful Life." *Mental Floss*. Last modified December 18, 2020. https://www.mentalfloss.com/article/60792/25-wonderful-facts-about-its-wonderful-life..

14 "Why Do We Make Fun of Fruitcake?" Martha Stewart. Last modified September 20, 2017, https://www.marthastewart.com/1520842/fruitcake-not-joke-why-we-eat-christmas.

15 Erika Wolf, "15 Fun Facts About Fruitcake," *Mental Floss*, last modified April 18, 2016, https://www.mentalfloss.com/article/60595/15-fun-facts-about-fruitcake.

16 Begley, Sarah, and Julia Lull. "How 'The Nutcracker' Colonized American Ballet." Time. Last modified December 24, 2014. https://time.com/3640792/nutcracker-american-history.

17 "How the Grinch Stole Christmas! (animated) Quotes...Movie Quotes Database," Movie Quotes Database, accessed November 7, 2022, https://www.moviequotedb.com/movies/how-the-grinch-stole-christmas-animated.html.

18 Campbell, Christopher. "10 Amazing Fun Facts: 'The Polar Express'." Fandango. Last modified December 10, 2019. https://www.fandango.com/movie-news/10-amazing-fun-facts-the-polar-express-753963.

19 Taylor, Justin. "The True Story of Pain and Hope Behind "I Heard the Bells on Christmas Day"." The Gospel Coalition. Last modified December 21, 2014. https://www.thegospelcoalition.org/blogs/justin-taylor/the-story-of-pain-and-hope-behind-i-heard-the-bells-on-christmas-day/.

20 Klein, Christopher. "8 Things You May Not Know About "Jingle Bells"." HISTORY. Last modified August 31, 2018. https://www.history.com/news/8-things-you-may-not-know-about-jingle-bells.

21 Allen, Kelly, and Jessica Cherner. "80 DIY Gifts to Make for Your Friends and Family This Holiday Season." House Beautiful. Last modified November 11, 2022. https://www.housebeautiful.com/entertaining/holidays-celebrations/g2789/diy-christmas-gifts/.

22 "Christmas Town U.S.A. Turns on Its 'scaled Back' Lights." Https://www.wbtv.com. Last modified December 1, 2020. https://www.wbtv.com/2020/12/01/christmas-town-usa-turns-its-scaled-back-lights-tuesday-mcadenville/.

23 "27 Best Christmas Light Displays in the US." Attractions of America. Accessed August 14, 2022. https://www.attractionsofamerica.com/travel/top-dazzling-holiday-light-displays-america.php.

24 "Angel Tree." The Salvation Army. Accessed December 10, 2022. https://saangeltree.org/.

25 Candy Cane History & Legends." Spangler Candy | Family Owned Candy Company Since 1906. Accessed January 30, 2023. https://www.spanglercandy.com/our-brands/candy-canes/legends#:~:text=It%20wasn%27t%20until%20the,of%20pure%20white%20hard%20candy.

26 Hucklebridge, Melanie. "True Stripes: Interesting Facts About Candy Canes." Where Y'at New Orleans. Last modified December 23, 2020. https://www.whereyat.com/true-stripes-interesting-facts-about-candy-canes.

27 "National Ugly Sweater Day." National Today. Last modified December 14, 2021, https://nationaltoday.com/national-ugly-sweater-day/.

28 Staff, Farmers' A. "The Legend of the Poinsettia." Farmers' Almanac—Plan Your Day. Grow Your Life. Last modified October 4, 2022. https://www.farmersalmanac.com/poinsettia-legend-facts-trivia.

29 Mozo, Jessica. "8 Fun Facts to Know About Poinsettias." National FFA Organization. Last modified February 11, 2021. https://www.ffa.org/ffa-new-horizons/8-fun-facts-to-know-about-poinsettias.

30 Ly, Linda. "The Real (and Weird) Reason We Kiss Under the Mistletoe." Garden Betty. Last modified December 28, 2020. https://www.gardenbetty.com/the-curious-history-of-the-mistletoe-its-more-than-just-the-kissing-plant/.

31 "St. Nicholas Church, Myra: Photos." St. Nicholas Center. Accessed August 2, 2022. https://www.stnicholascenter.org/around-the-world/customs/turkey/myra-church.

32 W., Audrey. "The Little-Known History of the Caroling Tradition." Arcadia Publishing | Local and Regional History Books. Accessed September 11, 2022. https://www.arcadiapublishing.com/Navigation/Community/Arcadia-and-THP-Blog/November-2018/The-Little-Known-History-of-the-Caroling-Tradition.

33 Fox, Alison. "More Than 109 Million Americans Expected to Travel for the Holidays, According to AAA." Travel + Leisure. Last modified December 15, 2021. https://www.travelandleisure.com/travel-news/us-holiday-travel-data-aaa.

34 Black, Rosemary. "The Wellesley Cookie Exchange 40 Year Tradition." Parade. Last modified December 14, 2011. https://parade.com/120058/rosemaryblack/14-wellesley-cookie-exchange/.

35 Britannica, T. Editors of Encyclopaedia. "the Salvation Army." Encyclopedia Britannica, September 13, 2022. https://www.britannica.com/topic/Salvation-Army.

36 Kellner, Mark A. "Despite Reported Pushback, Salvation Army's Kettles Set Record in Recent Challenge." The Washington Times. Last modified December 14, 2021. https://www.washingtontimes.com/news/2021/dec/14/salvation-armys-kettles-set-record-recent-challeng/.

37 Jeunesse, Marilyn L. "13 Surprising Things You Might Not Know About 'Elf.'" Insider. Last modified December 8, 2020. https://www.insider.com/elf-fun-facts-2018-12.

38 Puchko, Kristy. "21 Fun Facts About Elf." *Mental Floss*. Last modified December 8, 2021. https://www.mentalfloss.com/article/60421/21-things-you-might-not-know-about-elf.

39 Mauro, JP. "The World's Largest Nativity Scene is in Alicante, Spain." Aleteia. Last modified December 4, 2020. https://aleteia.org/2020/12/04/the-worlds-largest-nativity-scene-is-in-alicante-spain.

40 "Civil War Era Christmas Traditions—The Pickle." CivilWarTalk. Accessed November 7, 2022. https://civilwartalk.com/threads/civil-war-era-christmas-traditions-the-pickle.92901/.

41 "The Mysterious Tradition of Hiding a Pickle on Christmas Trees." Atlas Obscura. Last modified December 6, 2022. https://www.atlasobscura.com/articles/mysterious-christmas-pickle-tradition-hiding-german.

42 Mossolle, Maitlynn. "This Small MI Town Is The Christmas Pickle Capital Of The World." 94.9 WMMQ. Last modified December 16, 2019. https://wmmq.com/this-small-mi-town-is-the-christmas-pickle-capital-of-the-world/.

43 D'Arminio, Aubry. "4 Hot Facts You Need to Know About the Original Yule Log." TV Insider. Last modified December 24, 2017. https://www.tvinsider.com/652997/4-facts-need-to-know-the-original-yule-log.

44 Hendrix, Steve. "A child calling Santa reached NORAD instead. Christmas Eve was never the same." *The Washington Post*, December 24, 2018. https://www.washingtonpost.com/history/2018/12/24/child-calling-santa-reached-norad-instead-christmas-eve-was-never-same.

45 Spyker, Marisa. "How Matching Family Pajamas Became a Viral Holiday Tradition." Southern Living. Last modified July 8, 2022. https://www.southernliving.com/holidays-occasions/christmas/family-tradition-christmas-pjs.

46 Morris, Michele K. "A Visit from St. Nicholas." Heroes, Heroines, and History. Last modified December 26, 2015. https://www.hhhistory.com/2015/12/a-visit-from-st-nicholas.html.

We wish you a merry Christmas